Leading Lawyers'
Case for the
RESURRECTION

Also by Ross Clifford

Leading Lawyers' Case for the
RESURRECTION

Ross Clifford

An imprint of 1517. The Legacy Project

Third Edition, January 2015

© 1991, 1996, 2015 Ross Clifford

Clifford, Ross, 1951-
      Leading Lawyers' Case for the Resurrection

      ISBN 978-1-945500-04-6
      (Previously published by Canadian Institute for Law,
      Theology, & Public Policy, Inc. under ISBN 0-896363-02-4
      in 1996 and by Albatross Books Pty Ltd under ISBN
      0-86760-127-2 in 1991)

      1. Jesus Christ – Historicity
      2. Jesus Christ – Resurrection
      3. Jesus Christ - Resurrection - Biblical teaching
      4. Bible. N.T. Gospels - Evidences, etc.
      5. Dead Sea scrolls - Relation to the New Testament
      I. Title

NRP Books, an imprint of 1517 The Legacy Project (www.1517legacy.com)
P.O. Box 54032
Irvine, California 92619-4032

NRP Books is committed to packaging and promoting the finest
content for fueling a new Lutheran Reformation. We promote the
defense of the Christian Faith, confessional Lutheran theology,
vocation and civil courage.

Contents

*For my Russian friends
and those whose love, patience and
assistance made this book possible*

*'The Christianity of the future must be a religion of reason
as well as of faith, else it cannot and will not endure
the shocks of time, or survive the onward march
of the soul.'*

WALTER MARION CHANDLER
lawyer, 1867–1935

Introduction

MY LIFE WAS AT THE CROSSROADS. For the first time I was seriously questioning my parents' faith. This was not altogether unusual, considering my background: Christian home, church school, strong local church. Hardly surprisingly, I needed to integrate this hand-me-down faith and make it my own! But now I was alone in my study, a lawyer training for the ministry, asking whether it was all true.

Is Christ really God? Did he rise from the dead, or was the Jesus story just a myth developed by the early church? The concerns that were ripping at my soul had their source in my required reading. I was paralysed by doubt! Was it all a waste of time? Should I leave my theological training and resume my practice of law? I knew I could not continue on my present course if my doubts were unresolved.

I went for a quiet stroll around the college and, as I passed a hastily erected secondhand bookstall, my eyes were drawn to a book called *The Law above the Law*[1]. I thought this might be worth buying. I paid the twenty-cent-giveaway price, found a quiet spot and turned the soiled pages. The result was that for the first time in months, I became fully committed to the whole notion that God was in Christ and was able to return contentedly to my theological studies.

The book that changed my life contained the views of two prominent lawyers, Dr John Warwick Montgomery and Professor Simon Greenleaf, on the first four books of the New Testament: Matthew, Mark, Luke and John — the Gospels. They claimed that they were reliable historical documents and that the authors were witnesses who would be believed in any court of law when they declared Christ lived, died and rose again.

How often have you heard these statements: faith in God is a leap in the dark; faith is for the tender-hearted, not the tough-minded; no-one who is intelligent believes. Such statements, I have found, are simply not true. Those who take time to investigate the claims of Christianity will discover that they are based on strong, reliable evidence.

In this book I will summarise some of the research by leading lawyers who have defended their faith in Jesus Christ. Included is the evidence of the two who had such an impact on me. I will then evaluate pertinent facts that have drawn them, and others, to Jesus. The advocates discussed here know what it is to struggle with doubt, hardship and failure. They span some 150 years, come from diverse backgrounds and represent many countries — including the USA, Ireland, England, Guyana, Australia.

This indicates that a legal defence of the Christ event is not confined to any one group or period of time. We can go back as far as the Dutchman Hugo Grotius (1583–1645), for example, the father of international law, who was a foremost defender of the Christian faith.

Why listen to the lawyers?

Unlike more subjective, speculative religions, Christianity is a religion based on historical facts. Lawyers, unlike philosophers and theologians, have the skills to assess the reliability of documents such as ones in which the Jesus story is told. Daily they are called on to 'sift' evidence. They are a voice to be listened to as we try and decide on the reliability of the Jesus story and his claims about the ultimate questions of life.

These ultimate questions are bound up in core Christian beliefs. They are found in the Bible and a general summary is encapsulated in this ancient Christian statement, the Apostles' Creed:

> I believe in God the Father Almighty, maker of heaven and earth. And in Jesus Christ, his only Son, our Lord: who was conceived by the Holy Spirit, born of the virgin Mary; suffered under Pontius Pilate; was crucified, dead, and buried; he descended into hell. The third day he rose again from the dead; he ascended into heaven, and is seated at the right hand of God the Father Almighty. From there he shall come to judge the living and the dead. I believe in the Holy Spirit; the holy catholic [Christian universal] church, the communion of saints; the forgiveness of sins; the resurrection of the body; and the life everlasting, Amen.

Whilst what the Creed says about God the Father, the Holy Spirit, the church and judgment are important, the strategic words are 'the third day he arose again from the dead'. If Jesus was resurrected he is the one to follow. He must be greater than Lenin or Marx, Mohammed or Buddha as, unlike them, he is not a prisoner of the tomb.

There is more, however.

If Christ rose, that points to his being 'God in the flesh'. During his earthly ministry, Jesus said that his resurrection would be the sign of his deity.[2] The apostle Paul wrote in Romans 1, verse 4 that Jesus 'was declared with power to be the Son of God by his resurrection from the dead: Jesus Christ our Lord'. Sir Norman Anderson, eminent law professor, explains it this way:

> During Jesus' earthly life his disciples clearly regarded him as teacher, prophet and Messiah and yet essentially human (as, in a very real sense, he truly was). It was only after the resurrection that they began to identify him — in some way they could not fully understand or explain — with the Lord God of Israel; to feel at liberty to worship him and address him in prayer, and to think of him as the 'Lord Jesus'. The evidence for the fact that he did indeed rise again is, in my judgment, quite extraordinarily strong...[3]

Certainly, the resurrection is an appropriate proof of deity. Anyone who eternally defeats mankind's ultimate foe — death — deserves to be worshipped. Also, Jesus' death takes on a new significance. If he has offered proof of deity by his resurrection, we can trust his claims that his crucifixion would pay the penalty for our sins and bring us eternal life.[4]

Principles and methodology
In the pages that follow, the case for Jesus' life, death and resurrection will be developed. Like a

jury, let us come with an open mind, putting aside prejudices and remembering the following principles:

* *Evidence does not bring one hundred per cent certainty.* All decisions in life are founded on probability. However, the evidence gives us information so we can make wise decisions. So when asking whether we should commit ourselves to Christ, we should determine if the *weight* of evidence is in favour of the Jesus story or not.

  The weighing of evidence is a process judges and juries undertake every day. In civil cases, they work on the preponderance of evidence — in other words, on which argument has the greater weight of evidence in support. As Joseph Butler (1697–1752) said, nothing could be probable to an infinite intelligence, 'but to us, probability is the very guide of life'.[5]

* *To make a decision against the evidence is to commit intellectual suicide and be intellectually dishonest.* If the evidence disproves a proposition, we are likely to dispense with the proposition. And if the evidence proves it, integrity requires we back it.

* *Doubts fold in the face of facts.* But facts need to be stated and evidence needs to be examined. That is our task here.

Now let us call the lawyers to the witness box to help us discover the truth about Jesus.

Endnotes:

1. John Warwick Montgomery, *The Law above the Law*, Bethany, 1973
2. Matthew 27, verses 39 to 43; Mark 2, verses 1 to 12; John 2, verses 18 to 22; John 10, verse 30 and John 20, verses 26 to 28
3. Sir Norman Anderson, *The Fact of Christ: Some of the Evidence*, IVP, 1979, p.15
4. Matthew 26, verse 28; John 3, verses 14 and 15
5. Joseph Butler, *The Analogy of Religion, Natural and Revealed, to the Constitution and Course of Nature*, rpt, George Bell, 1893, p.73

1

Judge Edmund H. Bennett:
A model lawyer

Who wrote the Gospels?

IT IS APPROPRIATE our first lawyer should be the American, Judge Bennett, as he was one of the most respected and loved lawyers of his day. He was born in Manchester, Vermont in 1824 and died in Boston in 1898.

Educated in his native state, he graduated from the University of Vermont at Burlington in the class of 1843. Edmund Bennett then pursued his legal studies in the office of his father, becoming a member of the bar of Vermont in 1847.

In 1848, there was a move to Taunton, Massachusetts where he began the active practice of law. At the relatively young age of thirty-four, he was appointed a judge of the Probate and Insolvency Court for Bristol County, Commonwealth of Massachusetts. Legal education was an area of interest to Judge Bennett. From 1870 to 1872 he occupied a position as lecturer at the prestigious law school, at Harvard University. In 1872, he received the degree of Doctor of Laws from the University of Vermont. Dr Bennett was also closely connected with the Boston University school of law from its commencement and was the dean there from 1876 until his death twenty-two years later.Judge Bennett was a very keen 'community man'. He was elected the first mayor of Taunton in 1865 and was re-elected for the following two years. It is claimed he was known personally or by name by nearly every lawyer in New England and also by many of those in other states.

At the memorial service in honour of Judge Bennett, the following resolution was adopted by the Bristol County bar:

> In the death of Edmund H. Bennett, our bar has suffered a grievous loss, a loss recognised and shared in by the whole community... With a wonderful grasp of details, he combined a profound insight into legal principle. He was not the slave of precedent, and ever sought to establish his conclusions in the spirit of justice and equity... As a skilled advocate, wise counsellor, upright judge, patriotic citizen and virtuous man, he has left his lasting impression for good on the minds and hearts of his generation. To us especially, his brothers in the law, his life has been and must continue to be an inspiration and benediction.[1]

Even allowing for the rhetoric that is common in any eulogy, it is apparent that Judge Bennett was a man of ability, had the respect of his peers and exercised great influence. Judge Bennett wrote or edited, alone or in company with others, in excess of one hundred volumes. His works were diverse, the best known being *English Law and Equity Reports* and an edition of Justice Story's *Leading Criminal Cases.*

For our purposes, his most interesting book is *The Four Gospels from a Lawyer's Standpoint.*[2] It is based on his oral defence of the Gospels, which he frequently presented before public audiences and which was published posthumously in 1899. In it he examined whether the Gospels of Matthew, Mark, Luke and John are forgeries or fakes. He concluded that they are not.

Who wrote the Gospels?

Judge Bennett supports the traditional authorship of the Gospels. He focuses not on what history says, but on what lawyers call the 'intrinsic evidence' of the material. He applies his analytical mind to each Gospel to see if there is internal evidence that gives us clues as to who wrote them. He finds these clues lead to Matthew, Mark, Luke and John.[3]

Before we examine Judge Bennett's evidence, who were Matthew, Mark, Luke and John?

(a) *Matthew* was one of Jesus' twelve chosen disciples. His profession has been one of the most despised since the dawn of civilisation — that of a tax collector. He was also known by the name Levi.[4]

(b) *Mark* mixed in the company of the early Christian leaders. He went on a missionary journey with the apostle Paul and was a cousin of Barnabas,[5] another prominent character in the early church. Many scholars suggest the Bible implies that the Last Supper and the Easter resurrection appearances took place in one central location in Jerusalem, that being the home of Mark's mother.[6]

There is a tradition that the young man who fled naked from the garden of Gethsemane as Jesus was arrested was John Mark.[7]

Mark was in a position to record accurately the life of Christ. His story is even more trustworthy if, as I believe, he wrote as Peter's scribe. Peter was one of Jesus' chosen twelve disciples who had an interest in a fishing business.[8] He lived in Capernaum with his brother[9] and went on to be a stalwart of the early church.

(c) *Luke*, according to the apostle Paul, was a physician.[10] He was a travel companion of Paul. He also is the author of the book of Acts. Dr. E.M. Blaiklock, former professor of classics at the University of Auckland, New Zealand, says of Luke's book, 'the third Gospel. . . is the work of a first-rate historian.'[11] The late Sir William Ramsey, internationally regarded archaeologist, agrees:

> Luke is a historian of the first rank; not merely are his statements of fact trustworthy; he is possessed of the true historic sense. . . In short, this author should be placed along with the very greatest of historians.[12]

(d) *John*, too, was one of the chosen twelve. He, like Peter, was very close to Jesus, one of the inner three. His family name was Zebedee and he was prominent in the fishing industries around Capernaum.

The Gospels imply that his mother was Salome, who was also Jesus' aunt. This means John was an actual cousin of Christ. The terms 'the mother of Zebedee's sons' (Matthew), 'Salome' (Mark) and

'Jesus' mother's sister'(John) appear to be one and
the same person, but described differently by each
author.[13] Matthew and John are the type of witnesses lawyers love. They were eyewitnesses to the
story of Jesus, as was Peter for whom, I believe,
Mark writes.

Here is an outline of the evidence Judge Bennett
adopted for each of the Gospels.

❑ The intrinsic evidence

(a) *The book of Matthew* contains strong evidence for
Matthew's authorship. For example, whilst all the
Gospels have a number of stories about tax collec-
tors, Matthew is the only one that records the narrative of Jesus paying his own personal tax.[14]

Judge Bennett surmises:

> Why should Matthew be more likely to mention
> this particular fact than any other evangelist? When
> we remember that he was himself a tax-gatherer,
> and therefore especially interested in and observant
> of anything relating to his own profession, the
> answer is obvious.[15]

Judge Bennett also alludes to 'the dinner' mentioned in Matthew 9, verse 10. Although the previous verse narrates the call of Matthew to be a disciple of Christ, verse 10 does not indicate that the
feast that followed was in Matthew's home. The
parallel accounts in Mark and Luke do state it was
Matthew's residence.[16] Bennett believes this is a
sign that Matthew is the writer as, in all modesty, he
omits reference to himself and to the magnitude of
the feast.

It is interesting to note that some today feel Matthew may have been more of an editor than an author. Certainly, he appears to rely on Mark's Gospel and other sources. However, there is no reason why an eyewitness should not avail himself of sources that he knows are accurate. If Matthew is more of an editor, he still has added his own personal touches.

(b) *The book of Mark* contains a clue that suggests its authorship. The tradition of the early church is that it was Mark who wrote this Gospel for Christians in Rome and Italy. This Gospel alone mentions in detail the healing of the deaf and dumb mute and records Jesus' actual spoken word 'Ephphatha' (chapter 7, verse 34). The writer translates this Aramaic word as 'be opened'.

Judge Bennett's point is that this affirms the tradition that Mark was written for non-Jews, as an explanation of the local Aramaic word was necessary. Therefore, as Bennett implies, if the tradition as to the readership of the Gospel is internally verified, one can rely on the assertion of tradition that Mark is the author.

Peter, in my view, is a more dominant figure in Mark, failures and all, than in the other Gospels, suggesting he was the man behind the scenes. This is the impression many receive as they read the Gospel. Further, New Testament scholar C.H. Dodd observed that Peter's message in Acts 10, verses 34 to 43 has a similar structure to the chronology of the book of Mark. This substantiates a reliance by Mark on Peter's spoken word.[17]

(c) *The book of Luke* would be expected to have

medical emphases if Luke were the author, for he was a doctor. And we do have such evidence! All four Gospels record the incident where Peter cuts off the ear of the High Priest's servant. But Luke alone (chapter 22, verses 50 and 51) documents Jesus restoring the man's ear.

In addition, where Matthew and Mark speak of Peter's mother-in-law as having a fever, Luke diagnoses (chapter 4, verse 38) a *high* fever. Similarly Luke (chapter 5, verse 12) records Jesus as not just healing a leper, but a man *full* of leprosy. Judge Bennett confirms that passages like this endorse Lucan authorship.

It is also interesting to note that Luke (chapter 8, verse 43), unlike Mark (chapter 5, verse 26), makes no mention of the woman with the haemorrhage having spent all her money on doctors. Perhaps this is a case of professional etiquette!

(d) *The book of John* presents as a very honest, eyewitness account of a close acquaintance of Jesus. It is John's writing which gives us the moving stories of the marriage at Cana (chapter 2), the encounter with the Samaritan woman (chapter 4) and the raising from the dead of Jesus' good friend, Lazarus (chapter 11). It alone states (in chapter 11, verse 35) 'Jesus wept'.

Without doubt, the Gospel is the testimony of someone who knew Christ well. In fact, in chapter 21, verses 19 to 25, the author is called the disciple whom Jesus loved. Judge Bennett finds the personal nature of this book supports the author being the apostle John. The book of Mark (chapter 9, verses 2 to 7) shows that John was one of the 'inner circle' and he was possibly a cousin of Jesus. Who else would have been close enough to Christ to write these things and to be identified as the one Jesus loved?

In fact, I would go further. It could not be Peter: he is referred to in the third person in the Gospel. Or James, the other member of the 'inner circle', who died at an early date. By a process of elimination we are left with John.

❏ Other evidence on authorship

Judge Bennett's view on the authorship of the Gospels is amply supported by those who wrote shortly after the Gospels were written:

(a) *Irenaeus, Bishop of Lyons* studied under Polycarp, Bishop of Smyrna. Polycarp was a disciple of the apostle John who 'always taught what he learned from the apostles'.[18] Irenaeus, writing in about AD 180, noted:

> Matthew published his Gospel among the Hebrews [i.e. Jews] in their own tongue, when Peter and Paul were preaching the Gospel in Rome and founding the church there. After their departure, Mark, the disciple and interpreter of Peter, himself handed down to us in writing the substance of Peter's preaching. Luke, the follower of Paul, set down in a book the Gospel preached by his teacher. Then John, the disciple of the Lord, who also leaned on his breast, himself produced his Gospel while he was living at Ephesus in Asia.[19]

(b) *Papias, Bishop of Hierapolis,* confirms Irenaeus' view of the authorship of Matthew and Mark. Relying on information obtained from the 'elder', the apostle John, he wrote the following in AD 130:

> The Elder used to say this also: Mark, having been
> the interpreter of Peter, wrote down accurately all
> that [Peter] mentioned, whether sayings or doings
> of Christ; not, however, in order. For he was
> neither a hearer nor a companion of the Lord; but
> afterwards, as I said, he accompanied Peter, who
> adapted his teachings as necessity required, not as
> though he were making a compilation of the
> sayings of the Lord. So then Mark made no
> mistake, writing down in this way some things as
> [Peter] mentioned them; for he paid attention to this
> one thing, not to omit anything that he had heard,
> nor to include any false statement among them. . .
> Matthew recorded the oracles in the [Aramaic]
> tongue.[20]

(c) *The Muratorian Canon*, written from Rome in
about AD 190, supports Luke and John as the
authors of the third and fourth Gospels respectively:

> The third book of the gospel, that according to
> Luke, was compiled in his own name on Paul's
> authority by Luke the Physician, when after Christ's
> ascension Paul had taken him to be with him. . .
> The fourth book of the gospel is that of John, one of
> the disciples.[21]

We can be confident from the above evidence, I
believe, that history has preserved for us the
authors of the four Gospels. They are properly
named after Matthew, Mark (as Peter's scribe), Luke
and John.

A question in reply
The external evidence (historical references) and in-

ternal evidence (from the documents themselves) leads one to conclude Matthew, Mark (Peter's scribe), Luke and John were the creators of the Gospels, but certain modern scholars and sceptics ask: Is there sufficient evidence to justify this conclusion? A detailed response to the doubters of traditional authorship can be read in the writings of Dr E.M. Blaiklock and Dr Paul Barnett.[22] Both ably discuss the historical and literary evidence itself. But there is another point as well.

It is a principle of legal interpretation that one does not primarily rely on what some expert says hundreds of years later, but rather on what the document says and the comments of those who came from that time. Edward A. McDowell, professor emeritus of New Testament at Southeastern Baptist Seminary in North Carolina, when commenting on the authorship of the epistles of John, rightly observed:

It seems reasonable, in the absence of positive evidence to the contrary, to accept the testimony of the early church, who were closer to the scene by 1800 years than twentieth century scholars.[23]

Even if one still rejects some or all of the authors as being Matthew, Mark, Luke and John, one would *still* have to admit the writers were people close to the Jesus story and three testify as eyewitnesses. Though the evidence affirms traditional authorship, this does not mean the writers could not have relied on some common, respected sources — an admission Luke makes (chapter 1, verses 1 to 4). However, a prudent person will move with much more caution than some current biblical critics.

In this context, a fascinating case is *Deeks v Wells et al*. It concerned Florence Deeks of Toronto, Canada who submitted her manuscript, *The Web*, to the publishers, MacMillan. Some months later, H.G. Wells allowed MacMillan to publish his *Outline of History* and, in short, Deeks claimed Wells had plagiarised her work. Deeks called a number of literary critics to prove her claim, but the action failed in the Ontario Supreme Court. It was then dismissed by the Ontario Supreme Court, Appellate Division, and by the Privy Council (at that time the highest Court of Appeal in the British Commonwealth).

The case shows how difficult it is for literary critics to prove the nature of a source without strong, corroborating evidence. Critics who express their basically unsubstantiated views on the origins of the sources used in the Gospels, suggesting they emanated from the Essene/Qumran community and Gnostic writings, should take note.

This comment was made by one of the Appellate judges in the Deeks versus Wells case on some of the more adventurous testimony:

> I have no hesitation in agreeing with the learned trial judge (Raney, J.) in the utter worthlessness of this kind of evidence — it is almost an insult to common sense.[24]

Conclusion

We can conclude with conviction, I believe, that the Gospels were written by people close to Jesus, the evidence pointing to the traditional authors being

Matthew, Mark, Luke and John, who at times relied on common sources. The next question is whether their story has come down to us in the form of reliable historical documents.

Endnotes:

1. Conrad Reno, *Memoirs of the Judiciary and the Bar of New England for the Nineteenth Century, with a history of the Judicial System of New England*, I Century Memorial Publishing, 1900, p.12

2. Edmund H. Bennett, *The Four Gospels from a Lawyer's Standpoint*, Houghton, Mifflin, 1899. Photo-reproduced in *The Simon Greenleaf Law Review*, I, 1981–1982

3. Edmund H. Bennett, *op. cit.*, pp. 9-22

4. Matthew 9, verse 9; Matthew 10, verse 3

5. Colossians 4, verse 10

6. Mark 14, verse 15; Luke 22, verse 12; Luke 24, verse 33; Acts 1, verses 13 to 15; Acts 2, verse 41; Acts 12, verse 12

7. Mark 14, verses 51 and 52

8. Luke 5, verse 10

9. Mark 1, verse 29

10. Colossians 4, verse 14

11. E.M. Blaiklock, *Jesus Christ: Man or Myth*, Nelson, 1974, p.45

12. Cited in F.F. Bruce, *The New Testament Documents: Are they reliable?*, IVP, 1960, p.91

13. Matthew 27, verse 56; Mark 15, verse 40; Mark 16, verse 1; John 19, verse 25

14. Matthew 17, verses 26 and 27

15. Edmund H. Bennett, *op. cit.*, p.10

16. Mark 2, verse 15; Luke 5, verse 29

17. See Paul Barnett, *Is the New Testament History?*, Hodder and Stoughton, 1986, pp.85-87

18. Irenaeus, *Adversus haereses*, 3.3.4

19. *Ibid*, 3.1.1

20. Cited in Eusebius, *Historia ecclesiastica*, 3.39

21. J. Stevenson, *A New Eusebius*, SPCK, 1957, pp.144-145

22. E.M. Blaiklock, *op.cit.* and Paul Barnett, *op cit*

23. J. Allen Clifton (ed.), *The Broadman Bible Commentary*, 12, Broadman, 1972, p. 190

24. J.A. Riddell, *Deeks v Wells et al [1931], 4 D.L.R. at 541. See also [1930] D.L.R. 513-27.*

2

Dr John Warwick Montgomery:
A prominent scholar

Are the Gospels reliable, historical documents?

JOHN MONTGOMERY HAS MASTERED many disciplines, writing authoritatively on law, philosophy, history, theology, ethics and apologetics. He has an earned doctorate from the University of Chicago. His other doctorate is a story in itself. In a year (1963–1964) he learnt the French language, wrote a 1000-page thesis and was awarded a doctorate in theology at the University of Strasbourg, France.

Dr Montgomery has eight other earned degrees which he has received from tertiary institutions such as the University of California and the University of Essex. His Master of Philosophy in Law from the latter university was awarded for his thesis, *The Marxist Approach to Human Rights: Analysis and Critique.*

Human rights has proved to be one of Dr

Montgomery's passions and he has a diploma (cum laude) from the International Institute of Human Rights, Strasbourg. His book, *Human Rights and Human Dignity*, is a balanced and thorough introduction to and appraisal of the human rights movement. A second book, *Giant in Chains*, deals with recent events in Tiananmen Square, China.

Dr Montgomery has held academic posts at a number of strategic places of higher learning including the University of Chicago, Trinity Evangelical Divinity School and the International School of Law, Washington, DC. He was founding Dean of the Simon Greenleaf School of Law.

At present he is Professor of Law and Humanities at the University of Luton, England.

Although an American citizen, Dr Montgomery is more rightly an internationalist. He now resides in London and spends part of the year in Strasbourg, the capital of Alsace, and currently the seat of both the Council of Europe and the European Court of Human Rights. Dr Montgomery is one of the few lawyers who are admitted to practise in both the United States and England.

Further, his influence as an ordained Lutheran minister has extended well beyond his own native land. For example, he was one of the six evangelical scholars invited by the then Prime Minister, Menachem Begin, to the signing of the historic Israel/Egypt Peace Accord.

He became a Christian in 1949, whilst in his late teens. At the time he was a student at Cornell University, Ithaca, New York, majoring in philosophy. A fellow student challenged the young academic to seriously consider Jesus Christ. The evidence convicted John Montgomery and he accepted Christianity 'kicking and screaming'. It was not his idea!

Ever since this time, Montgomery has been challenging others with words such as these:

> Christian faith, alone among the religious claims of history, is able to stand in the dock and be vindicated evidentially. For only Christianity rests its case on the divine life, sacrificial death and miraculous resurrection of the incarnate God — events witnessed to by those who had direct contact with them and who in consequence 'knew the score'.[1]

In the area of defence of the Christian faith, evidential apologetics, Dr Montgomery has been most influential. His scholarly works have been the foundation for much of the writing of such popular apologists as Josh McDowell and Don Stewart. His own lighter treatises such as *History and Christianity* have had their own impact. Dr Montgomery, in a creative way, has brought historical tests and the legal method to the Gospels in order to determine their reliability and truth. As a result of his academic contribution he, like Simon Greenleaf, would have to be included in any work on legal apologists.

Dr Montgomery has authored and edited forty books, among them *Faith Founded on Fact* and *Jurisprudence: A Book of Readings*.[2]

Are the Gospels reliable, historical documents?
This question has perplexed many a mind. As most
of what we know about Jesus' life, death and resurrection is found in the Gospels, it is a vital question.

Dr Montgomery applies a threefold test to the
Gospels to determine if they are trustworthy. It is
the criteria used by military historian, C. Sanders.[3]
The three tests are: the bibliographical test, which
we shall call 'the transmission', the internal
evidence test and the external evidence test.

In a recorded public debate in Sydney between
Dr Montgomery and the sceptic, Melbourne lawyer
Mark Plummer, the debaters were asked to explain
their basis for accepting or rejecting the Gospels.
The packed audience comprising Christians,
atheists, agnostics and some other colourful characters listened attentively. John Warwick Montgomery relied on the above threefold test used in
general historiography and literary criticism. Mark
Plummer unveiled the bankruptcy of his brief by
not being able to bring with conviction any reliable
criteria.[4]

Using Montgomery's threefold test, I have as-
sembled the following evidence that points to the
reliability of the historical documents:

❏ **The bibliographical or transmission test**
As we do not have the originals, known as
autographs, of most writings from antiquity — the
Gospels included — we must show that the hand-
written copies we do have, known as manuscripts,
come to us accurately and that from them we can
reconstruct the original. Only then can we say such

a document is reliable. Here, it is helpful to look at the number of copies and their date of composition.

Bruce Metzger, Professor Emeritus of New Testament at Princeton Theological Seminary has indicated that there still exist close to 5,000 Greek New Testament manuscripts.[5] As well as these, there are 15,000 existing copies of the early Latin, Syrian, Coptic and other translations of the New Testament. As the church grew, more copies had to be made.

I believe the volume of manuscripts is important for three reasons:

(a) *If a large number of copies when cross-checked say substantially the same thing, they evidence a high level of reliability.* What we find is that the Gospel manuscripts do just this. Admittedly, there are a number of variants, but with so many manuscripts, this is to be expected. The variants do not affect any matter of history or doctrine.

Let's call scholar and New Testament expert Stephen Neill and hear what he says:

> We have a far better and more reliable text of the New Testament than of any other ancient work whatever, and the measure of uncertainty is really rather small.[6]

(b) *Having a number of variant copies and readings aids scholars in reconstructing the original document and determining what passages are authentic.*

(c) *The accuracy or otherwise of the copying of the manuscripts can be determined.* As the numerous manuscripts coincide in so many ways, this shows that the copying of the originals of Matthew, Mark, Luke and John must have been done meticulously by all concerned. The closeness of the thousands of manuscripts justifies Dr Montgomery's statement of confidence in the accuracy of the text:

> To express scepticism concerning the resultant text of the New Testament books. . . is to allow all of classical antiquity to slip into obscurity, for no documents of the ancient period are as well attested bibliographically as is the New Testament.[7]

As to the date of the Gospel manuscripts, Sir Frederick Kenyon, at one time principal librarian and director of the British Museum, states:

> In no other case is the interval of time between the composition of the book and the date of the earliest manuscripts so short as in that of the New Testament. The books of the New Testament were written in the latter part of the first century; the earliest extant manuscripts (trifling scraps excepted) are of the fourth century — say, from 250 to 300 years later. This may sound a considerable interval, but it is nothing to that which parts most of the great classical authors from their earliest manuscripts.

Some years later Sir Frederick reiterated his finding:

> The interval, then, between the dates of original composition and the earliest extant evidence becomes so small as to be in fact negligible, and the last foundation for any doubt that the scriptures have come down to us substantially as they were written has now been removed. Both the authenticity and the general integrity of the books of the New Testament may be regarded as finally established.[8]

The following are some of these existing manuscripts that Sir Frederick refers to. We may remember that, as they are 'early' copies, we can have confidence in them.

* *The Bodmer Papyri*, which has much of John and Luke, is dated AD 175 to 225.
* *Codex Vaticanus* has been stored in the vatican for over 500 years. It contains all of the New Testament and is dated AD 325 to 350.
* *Codex Sinaiticus* was found at Mount Sinai in 1844 and is now housed in the British Museum. It also contains the New Testament and is a fourth century manuscript.

As stated earlier, other literature from antiquity cannot match the Gospels as far as the number of manuscripts and their 'early' dates are concerned. The following list offers a sobering comparison:

Author	Date written	Earliest copy	Time span	Copies
Matthew, Mark, Luke and John	c.AD 60-80	AD 200 (Bodmer) AD 325 (Codex V)	140— 265 yrs	20,000
Caesar	100–40 BC	AD 900	1300 yrs	10
Plato (Tetralogies)	427–347 BC	AD 900	1327 yrs	7
Tacitus Annals (and minor works)	AD 100	AD 1100	1000 yrs	10
Pliny the Younger (History)	AD 61–113	AD 850	789 yrs	7
Aristotle	384–322 BC	AD 1100	1484 yrs	49+
Homer (Iliad)	c.850 BC	400 BC	450 yrs	643.[9]

A lawyer would feel that the evidence points to the fact that the Gospels have been accurately transmitted and from the copies we can reconstruct the originals. The number of manuscripts and their early dates confirm this.

❏ The internal evidence test

This test requires one to examine an alleged historical document to discover what it says about itself. In other words, is there internal evidence that it is trustworthy? This is an important test because, as Dr Montgomery says:

> historical and literary scholarship continues to follow Aristotle's dictum that the benefit of doubt is to be given to the document itself, not arrogated by the critic to himself.[10]

In other words, doubt the critic before you doubt the document.

The intrinsic evidence indicates that the Gospels are primary source material — that is, the author is either an eyewitness to the events he describes or someone who is in a position to collect firsthand reports. Lawyers recognise primary source material as the most trustworthy.

The evidence that the Gospels are primary source material includes these biblical passages:

> Many have undertaken to draw up an account of the things that have been fulfilled among us, just as they were handed down to us by those who from the first were eye-witnesses and servants of the word. Therefore, since I myself have carefully investigated everything from the beginning, it

seemed good also to me to write an orderly account for you, most excellent Theophilus, so that you may know the certainty of the things you have been taught.[11]

The man who saw it has given testimony, and his testimony is true. He knows that he tells the truth, and he testifies so that you also may believe.[12] We did not follow cleverly invented stories when we told you about the power and coming of our Lord Jesus Christ, but we were eyewitnesses of his majesty.[13]

We proclaim to you what we have seen and heard, so that you also may have fellowship with us. And our fellowship is with the Father and with his Son, Jesus Christ.[14]

❏ The external evidence test

Dr Montgomery deals with the external evidence test by asking this question: 'Do other historical materials confirm or deny the internal testimony provided by the documents themselves?'[15] He believes they support the Gospels and I produce the following in support of his conclusion:

* We have seen that the external historical writings of Papias and Irenaeus verify the Gospels' claim to be primary source materials, written by those close to Christ.

* If, as they present, the Gospels were written by disciples of Jesus, then they must have been completed by the end of the first century. Extra-biblical writings that substantiate this are the writings of Clement of Rome (c.AD 96) where we find citations that can fairly be said to come from Matthew, Mark and Luke and the Epistle of Barnabas (c.AD 70-130) which quotes directly from

Matthew 22, verse 14 and Mark 2, verse 17.

* The Gospels as alleged primary source material reflect on the life and conditions in first century Palestine. This background material has been corroborated by archaeology. Some examples of this are given in the next chapter.

*   *   *

The three tests, therefore, demonstrate that Matthew, Mark, Luke and John are reliable, historical documents. The criteria used here would expose fabrication. Dr Montgomery says:

Competent historical scholarship must regard the New Testament documents as coming from the first century and as reflecting primary-source testimony about the person and claims of Jesus.[16]

A question in reply

But is the evidence of the trustworthiness of the Gospels sufficient? In reply to this question raised in some books and commentaries, the prominent Graeco-Roman historian, A.N. Sherwin White, in his Sarum Lectures on 'Roman Society and Roman Law in the New Testament', stated:

It is astonishing that while Graeco-Roman historians have been growing in confidence, the twentieth-century study of the Gospel narratives, starting from no less promising material, has taken so gloomy a turn in the development of form criticism that the more advanced exponents of it apparently maintain — so far as an amateur can understand the matter — that the historical Christ is unknowable and the history of his mission cannot be written.

This seems very curious when one compares the case for the best-known contemporary of Christ, who like Christ is a well-documented figure — Tiberius Caesar. The story of his reign is known from four sources, the Annals of Tacitus and the biography of Suetonius, written some eighty or ninety years later, the brief contemporary record of Valleius Paterculus, and the third-century history of Cassius Dio. These disagree amongst themselves in the wildest possible fashion, both in major matters of political action or motive and in specific details of minor events. Everyone would admit that Tacitus is the best of all the sources, and yet no serious modern historian would accept at face value the majority of the statements of Tacitus about the motives of Tiberius. But this does not prevent the belief that the material of Tacitus can be used to write a history of Tiberius.[17]

As Sherwin-White implies, the Gospels do allow us to write a proper history of Jesus because they are admissible historical documents.

Endnotes:

1. John Warwick Montgomery, *Law and Gospel: A Study in Jurisprudence*, Christian Legal Society, 1978, p.36

2. John Warwick Montgomery, *Faith Founded on Fact*, Nelson, 1978; John Warwick Montgomery (ed.), *Jurisprudence: A Book of Readings*, International Scholarly Publishers, 1974; John Warwick Montgomery, *Human Rights and Human Dignity*, Zondervan/Probe, 1986; John Warwick Montgomery, *History and Christianity*, IVP, 1971; and John Warwick Montgomery, *Giant in Chains: China Today and Tomorrow* (German edition), Trobisch/Hänssler, 1991

3. See John Warwick Montgomery, *History and Christianity*, pp.23-40 and C. Sanders, *Introduction to Research in English Literary History*, Macmillan, 1952, p.143

4. John Warwick Montgomery and Mark Plummer, *Humanism or Christianity?*, 17 February 1986. For a report on the debate, see the *Sydney Morning Herald*, 19 February 1986, p.23

5. Bruce M. Metzger, *The Text of the New Testament*, Oxford University Press, 1968, pp.31-33

6. Stephen Neill, *The Interpretation of the New Testament*, Oxford University Press, 1964, p.78

7. John Warwick Montgomery, *Where is History Going?*, Bethany, 1969, p.46

8. Frederick Kenyon, *Handbook to the Textual Criticism of the New Testament*, 2nd ed., Macmillan, 1912, p.5 and Frederick Kenyon, *The Bible and Archaeology*, Harper, 1940, pp.288-289

9. For corroboration of this information see F.W. Hall, 'Manuscript Authorities for the Text of the Chief Classical Writers', in *Companion to Classical Text*, Clarendon Press, 1913, pp. 199-200

10. John Warwick Montgomery, *History and Christianity*, p.29

11. Luke 1, verses 1 to 4

12. John 19, verse 35

13. 2 Peter 1, verse 16

14. 1 John 1, verse 3

15. John Warwick Montgomery, op. cit., p.23

16. *Ibid*, p.34
17. A.N. Sherwin-White, *Roman Society and Roman Law in the New Testament*, rpt, Baker, 1978, pp.187-188

3

Professor Simon Greenleaf:
Leading expert on evidence

Do the Gospel writers speak the truth?

SIMON GREENLEAF WAS BORN in 1783 in New-
buryport, Massachusetts, USA. As a young man he
entered the law office of Ezekiel Whitman, later
Chief Justice of Maine, and under his tutelage was
prepared for a career in law. Simon Greenleaf
proceeded to practise law in a number of places in
what is now Maine and read widely in his chosen
discipline. He was thought to have a very bright future in law.

When the Maine Supreme Court was established
in 1820, Simon Greenleaf was appointed the court's
reporter. He held this position for some twelve
years and during this period he built up his own
legal practice until he was the foremost legal figure
in Maine. One observer says that attractive personality, profound legal knowledge and compelling
logic made him particularly effective'.[1]

In acknowledgment of his reputation and skills
as a remarkably accurate, concise court reporter,

Simon Greenleaf was offered, at the age of fifty, the Royall Professorship of Law in the Harvard Law School. He held this post for thirteen years and was greatly respected by his students who affectionately nicknamed him 'Old Green'. As a lecturer, he displayed the thoroughness and scholarly ability that had marked his professional life.

On the death of his friend and ally, Joseph Story, Simon Greenleaf replaced him as Dane Professor. Their work played a major part in the development of Harvard Law School's coveted reputation.

The fame of Simon Greenleaf and his influence on the law was not limited to his professorship. He personally prepared the original constitution adopted by the African colony of Liberia. In 1820, he was elected to the first Maine State legislature where he took a prominent role in implementing its initial legislation. In his work as a lawyer he appeared as Chief Counsel in a number of most important cases, such as the famous US Supreme Court case of *Charles River v Warren Bridge* (11 Peters 420 [1837]). Further, he became recognised as the foremost North American authority on common law evidence.

As a leading expert on evidence, he is a voice to be listened to, therefore, when he evaluates the witnesses' testimony concerning the death and resurrection of Jesus Christ.

Honours given Simon Greenleaf include a Doctor of Laws by Harvard in 1834, by Amherst in 1845 and by the University of Alabama in 1852. Although he never held a judgeship, Simon Greenleaf is one of the most important legal figures in recent history, ranking with Blackstone.

An affirmation of Professor Greenleaf's prowess originated from the other side of the Atlantic. The London Law Journal wrote in 1874:

> It is no mean honour to America that her schools of jurisprudence have produced two of the first writers and best esteemed legal authorities of this century — the great and good man, Judge Story, and his eminent and worthy associate, Professor Greenleaf. Upon the existing law of evidence (by Greenleaf) more light has shone from the New World than from all the lawyers who adorn the courts of Europe.[2]

Simon Greenleaf was a committed Christian. In his very busy schedule he found time to serve for many years as President of the Massachusetts Bible Society and was very supportive of foreign missions.

In 1842, his book *A Treatise on the Law of Evidence* was published. A second volume was added in 1846 and a third in 1853. In its final form, the series was regarded as a standard text giving rise to numerous later editions under successive editors. Citations of its text are still found in scholarly legal opinions. Whilst at Harvard, he wrote as well a number of other legal works.

Professor Greenleaf's most influential Christian writing is *The Testimony of the Evangelists Examined by the Rules of Evidence Administered in Courts of Justice*. It looks at the trial of Jesus, shows that the four Gospels are in harmony with each other and that their writers would be believed in a court of law. Greenleaf makes no apology for his endeavours:

If a close examination of the evidence of
Christianity may be expected of one class of men
more than another, it would seem incumbent upon
us who make the law of evidence one of our
peculiar studies. Our profession leads us to explore
the mazes of falsehood, to detect its artifices, to
pierce its thickest veils, to follow and expose its
sophistries, to compare the statements of different
witnesses with severity, to discover truth and
separate it from error.[3]

Are the Gospel writers to be believed?

In chapters 1 and 2 we have seen that the Gospels
were written by men who were eyewitnesses to the
Christ event or at least had first-hand information.
Their writings are recognised as historical. But how
can we be sure that their testimony is true? Is it not
possible they fabricated some of the stories that deal
with Jesus' life, death and resurrection?

Simon Greenleaf, relying on another famous
lawyer of his day, Thomas Starkie, sets out a rule for
determining whether witnesses are telling the
whole truth and nothing but the truth. This rule is
just as useful today:

The credit due to the testimony of witnesses
depends upon, firstly, their honesty; secondly, their
ability; thirdly, their number and the consistency of
their testimony; fourthly, the conformity of their
testimony with experience; and fifthly, the
coincidence of their testimony with collateral
circumstances.[4]

Simon Greenleaf then examined the evangelists
Matthew, Mark, Luke and John by these five tests.
His work in this regard has set a precedent. Many

fine lawyers such as Walter Chandler and Clarrie Briese have followed suit.[5] These tests are most appropriate in evaluating these Gospel witnesses.

❏ The first Greenleaf test:
Are the witnesses honest?

In other words, are they sincere, really saying what they believe to be true? As one reads the Gospels, one is constantly confronted by the writers' openness and sincerity. They even deal with issues such as the failures of the disciples, the harshness of some of Jesus' teachings and Christ's own sense of despair and anguish at the thought of death.

Professor Greenleaf's conviction is that Matthew, Mark, Luke and John are 'good men, testifying to that which they had carefully observed and considered, and well knew to be true'.[6] They hide nothing.

❏ The second Greenleaf test:
Have the witnesses ability?

Simon Greenleaf argues that the ability of witnesses to speak the truth depends on factors such as the opportunities the witnesses had to observe the facts at issue, the accuracy of their powers to evaluate what they saw and heard, and their mental capabilities to remember things.[7] This is how I see these three factors:

(a) *Matthew, John and Peter (Mark) as disciples had many opportunities to observe the events in Jesus' life.* John records the execution of Jesus and confirms his own presence there.[8] The evidence points to Peter also being present at Jesus' trial and crucifixion.[9]

John and Peter went to the empty tomb (John chapters 20 and 21) and all three saw the resurrected Christ.

(b) *Luke as a physician and Matthew as a tax collector were in occupations that called for exactness in reports and evaluations.* They could be relied upon in their assessment.

(c) *There is absolutely no reason to question the mental capabilities of our four witnesses.* Lawyer Walter Chandler states:

> the writings themselves indicate extraordinary mental vigour, as well as cultivated intelligence. The Gospels of Luke and John, moreover, reveal that elegance of style and lofty imagery which are the invariable characteristics of intellectual depth and culture. The 'ignorant fisherman' idea is certainly not applicable to the Gospel writers. . . The fact that the Gospels were written in Greek by Hebrews indicated they were not entirely illiterate.[10]

❏ The third Greenleaf test:
Are there sufficient witnesses and are they consistent?

The number of witnesses in this case is sufficient to satisfy any court. As to the consistency of the testimony of the Gospel writers, Simon Greenleaf writes:

> There is enough of a discrepancy to show that there could have been no previous concert among them; and at the same time such substantial agreement as to show that they all were independent narrators of the same great transaction.[11]

By discrepancy, Greenleaf means the witnesses present their case in their own form and style. This is an important element in verifying the authenticity of witnesses.

❑ **The fourth Greenleaf test:**
Does the testimony of the witnesses conform to our experience?

Some say this is the Christian's Achilles' heel. The disciples speak of miracles and a resurrection and such do not conform with normal life experiences. Who's seen a miracle? A good point! However, for a lawyer there is a twofold problem with this:

(a) *It fails to appreciate that many people believe they have experienced the supernatural* whether it be in guidance, healing, miraculous protection or whatever. Belief in and experience of the supernatural is most common and therefore miracles are consistent with some human experience.

(b) *This test is not an absolute.* It is called by some authorities the 'incredible assertion test'. It rightly reminds one to be cautious if the testimony appears outrageous. However, if the facts demand a certain finding, then so be it, even though the testimony might be unusual. One must still go with the facts.

Our expert on evidence, Professor Greenleaf, says of the testimony about the miracles of Jesus:

> In every case of healing, the previous condition of the sufferer was known to all; all saw his instantaneous restoration; and all witnessed the act of Jesus in touching him, and heard his words. All these, separately considered, were facts, plain and simple in their nature, easily seen and fully

comprehended by persons of common capacity and observation. If they were separately testified to, by different witnesses of ordinary intelligence and integrity, in any court of justice, the jury would be bound to believe them; and a verdict, rendered contrary to the uncontradicted testimony of credible witnesses to any of these plain facts, separately taken, would be liable to be set aside, as a verdict against evidence.[12]

❑ **The fifth Greenleaf test:**

Does the testimony of the witnesses coincide with contemporaneous facts and circumstances?

This is the chief test applied to the written evidence of witnesses who for various reasons cannot be called to the witness stand. Matthew, Mark, Luke and John pass this test. I believe they speak accurately about the geography, history and sociological factors of their day.

Let us look at two examples:

(a) *The pavement.* John records that Jesus' Roman trial was at a place known by this name.[13] This trial is important in the story. If the pavement could be shown not to exist, one could ask if the whole trial account is fabrication. The pavement has been recently discovered.

(b) *The Pool of Bethesda.* This is mentioned in John 5, verses 1 to 15, but is not referred to in any other historical document. It has now been located with reasonable certainty.

It is interesting to note that dishonest witnesses tend to be very guarded in what they say. They avoid detail as they know the more they say, the more likely it is that they will be found out. In contrast, honest witnesses are refreshingly open. Matthew, Mark, Luke and John are in the latter category. They supply much information which can be cross-checked with what we know of life in those days. And their statements have been confirmed by the evidence.

Professor Simon Greenleaf believes the evidence indicates that Matthew, Mark, Luke and John pass this five-point test. I will now expose the witnesses to further tests.

❏ The Montgomery perjury tests

Dr Montgomery in his book, *Human Rights and Human Dignity*, applies a fourfold test for exposing knowingly given false testimony — perjury — to Matthew, Mark, Luke and John. His criteria are based on the work of modern legal scholars and authorities, McCloskey and Schoenberg.[14] Some of this perjury material is similar to the Greenleaf 'tests' and need not be repeated, except for the first two:

(a) *Are there internal defects in the witness himself?* Is there a personality disorder, criminal record or past history that would cause one to hold that the witness is inherently untrustworthy?

Now the Gospel writers are honest enough to admit human frailty and, on occasions, like most of us, they fail under pressure, but certainly there is no evidence of major defects such as their being habitual liars. If there were internal defects, the early critics of Christianity would surely have picked them up!

(b) *Are there external defects in the witness himself?*

That is, does the witness have any motives to fal-
sify? I feel Matthew, Mark, Luke and John would
have gained no financial or other material benefit
from lying. There was no status in being a leader of
a new, small sect. Further, they faced persecution
from the Jewish and Roman authorities for sharing
about Christ. They had everything to lose and nothing to gain.

❏ The embellishment test

On occasions witnesses, for various reasons, are
prone to exaggerate. Such witnesses are guilty of
embellishment and, if they are 'found out', their testimony is viewed as unreliable.

Some people suggest that the Gospel testimony
is full of embellishment. They base this assertion on
the fact that the Gospels were not written until some
years after the death of Christ and therefore as the
story of Jesus was told and retold, it must have become grander and more fanciful. As one examines
the Gospel testimony, such evidence as the following strongly mitigates against embellishment:

(a) *There is no confrontation of the historical issues that
concerned the church at the time Matthew, Mark, Luke
and John wrote.* Issues like whether Christians need
to be circumcised, the nature of the Godhead and
the role of the Old Testament law and freedom in
the Spirit are not treated.

These topics and others certainly occupied Paul's
thoughts in his letters. If our witnesses were open
to embellishment, they would have put words into
Jesus' mouth so as to address these issues. That
would have added weight to their writings and

made them 'relevant' to their day.

(b) *The Gospel writers are most honest about the tough teaching of Jesus and the failures of his disciples.* When there is embellishment, one expects such things to be covered up.

(c) *The Gospel writers sound like actual 'on the spot' eyewitnessess of the life, death and resurrection of Jesus.*

(d) *Many language scholars hold that in the Gospels it is clear that Aramaic expressions undergird the Greek.* Even though Jesus no doubt spoke in the common language of his people, Aramaic, the Gospels are written in Greek. Clearly the writers are trying to transcribe the actual teachings of Jesus and are not supplying their own embellished thoughts or paraphrase.[15]

❏ The Givens bias test

Richard A. Givens is another modern authority on the question of truth-telling. Givens suggests one should determine if a witness has an obvious bias which he will have to admit.[16] If that is so, one can then 'attack' the witness's objectivity and, if he fails this, his trustworthiness. This test should be applied to all witnesses.

In the case of the Gospel writers, there is no doubt they had good reason to be biased. They loved Jesus and three of them knew him very well. This would be admitted. However, an 'attack' on their testimony shows they wrote free of bias.

Walter Chandler in his apologetic agrees, noting in support the witnesses' impartial description of the insidious trial of Jesus, their generous approach to the cruel and unjust Pilate, their desire to simply record facts and their language, which is free of prejudices and fanaticism.[17]

A lawyer often finds it hard to tell if someone is telling the truth. There is no difficulty with the Gospel writers as they pass the Greenleaf, perjury, embellishment and bias tests.

A question in reply

Even if one admits the Gospels were written by decent, truthful folk, isn't it a fact that they did not record their story until years after the resurrection of Christ? Would we then not expect the memories of Matthew, Mark, Luke and John to be jaded?

In response to concerns such as this, I suggest a number of factors be kept in mind:

(a) *The Gospels were written within twenty to forty years of the death of Christ.* This is confirmed by respected New Testament scholar, J.A.T. Robinson, who notes there is no reference to the Jewish-Roman War of AD 66–70 in the New Testament and that would indicate it was written before that date.[18] William F. Albright, late W.W. Spence Professor of Semitic languages at John Hopkins University, is slightly more conservative, but just as affirming:

> In my opinion, every book of the New Testament was written by a baptised Jew between the forties and the eighties of the first century AD (very probably some time between AD 50 and 75).[19]

A twenty to forty year 'gap' between historical events and the recording of them is not unusual. For example, Alexander the Great died in 323 BC and scholars rely on the Greek historian Arrian and his treatise *Anabasis* for much of their information about Alexander's military campaigns. Arrian put pen to paper hundreds of years after the death of his subject. Yet who would doubt the story of Alexander the Great?

(b) *Jews in the time of Christ were trained to commit things to memory as they did not have the accessibility to books that we do.* Even today in the Middle East are found people who can recite large sections of the Old Testament. A gap in time between the Gospel events and the recording of them is not, therefore, likely to produce an unreliable record. Dr Montgomery affirms:

> We know from the Mishra that it was a Jewish custom to memorise a rabbi's teaching, for a good pupil was like 'a plastered cistern that loses not a drop' [Mishna Aboth, II.8]. And we can be sure that the early church, impressed as it was with Jesus, governed itself by this ideal.[20]

(c) *Most of us have good memories.* We can recall vividly important events that took place in our lives many years ago. Who can forget their marriage day, death of a loved one or some major period in their earthly journey?

(d) *Prominent lawyer, Sir Norman Anderson, holds that twenty-five to forty years is not a problem.* He draws our attention to three points:

> Much of Jesus' teaching must have been comparatively easy to remember in considerable detail — vivid miracles for example.
> Some of the teaching of Jesus may well have been jotted down in his lifetime.

If we date 1 Corinthians about AD 55, then some three hundred or more people who claimed actually to have seen the risen Christ were alive at that date, and several of the leading apostles were still living (cf. 1 Corinthians chapter 15). Thus a large number of eyewitnesses of the ministry of Jesus and some of the apostles themselves were in a position to contribute to, verify and check the oral traditions available to the evangelists and also, as many would claim, at least the earliest of the written records.[21]

This last point is a good one. If the evangelists' memories had let them down, someone would have told us. All the evidence outlined in this chapter indicates that Matthew, Mark, Luke and John are telling the truth.

Endnotes:

1. *Dictionary of American Biography*, VII, p.583
2. Cited in Irwin H. Linton, *A Lawyer Examines the Bible*, W.A. Wilde, 1943, p. 36
3. Simon Greenleaf, *The Testimony of the Evangelists*, rpt, Baker, 1984, p.vii
4. *Ibid*, p.28
5. See Appendices 1 and 2
6. Simon Greenleaf, *op.cit.*, p.31
7. *Ibid*, pp.31-32
8. John chapter 19, verses 16 to 37
9. Matthew 26, verses 56 to 75; Luke 23, verse 49
10. Walter M. Chandler, *The Trial of Jesus from a Lawyer's Standpoint*, I, Federal Book Co., 1925, p.19
11. Simon Greenleaf, *op.cit.*, p.32
12. *Ibid*, pp.41-42
13. John 19, verse 13
14. John Warwick Montgomery, *Human Rights and Human Dignity*, Zondervan/Probe, 1986, pp.140-144. See also Patrick L. McCloskey and Richard L. Schoenberg, *Criminal Law Advocacy*, 5, Matthew Bender, 1984
15. See John Benton, *Is Christianity True?*, Evangelical Press, 1988, pp.64-66
16. Richard A. Givens, *Advocacy: The Art of Pleading a Cause*, Shepard's/McGraw-Hill, 1980, pp. 69-90
17. Chandler, *op.cit.*, pp.19-25
18. John A.T. Robinson, *Redating the New Testament*, Westminster Press, 1976, pp.86-117
19. William F. Albright, Interview for *Christianity Today*, 18 January 1963
20. John Warwick Montgomery, *History and Christianity*, IVP, 1971, pp. 37-38
21. Norman Anderson, *The Teaching of Jesus*, IVP, 1983, pp.20, 18 and 21

4

Sir Robert Anderson:
The 'Jack the Ripper' detective

Do the Gospel writers complement each other?

SIR ROBERT ANDERSON HAD A most remarkable life.
Born in 1841 in Dublin, Ireland, he was educated
privately in France and his city of birth. His father
became Crown Solicitor for Dublin. At eighteen, he
entered Trinity College, Dublin, and in 1862
graduated Bachelor of Arts.

At the same time he was pursuing law, and his
hours of study were rewarded with him becoming a
Doctor of Laws from Trinity College in 1875. As a
student, Sir Robert never allowed 'the books' to be
his sole passion as this diary entry of 1861 testifies:
'Read for five hours; cricket.'[1]

In 1863, Sir Robert was called to the Irish Bar,
having done all that was necessary to be admitted
as a barrister-lawyer and successfully practised on
the court circuit around Ireland. He was admitted
to the English Bar, although he never practised in
England.

Historical events were to play a part in a career

change. The Irish Republican Brotherhood (Fenian Society) in 1865 began to increase its drive for an independent Irish state.

At that time no secret service existed in Dublin and someone was needed to collate material on these 'freedom fighters'. Government sources entrusted this to Sir Robert who, as a lawyer and son of the Crown Solicitor of Dublin, had the necessary contacts and skills. Sir Robert had for a short time joined the secret service. This led him in 1867 to move to London and to join the Home Office, a government department that administers domestic affairs, police, public services and the like. Sir Robert's first task at the Home Office was to take charge of Irish business.

Sir Robert's commitment to serving the people led to another interesting career opportunity. In 1888, he was appointed Assistant Commissioner of London's metropolitan police, Scotland Yard. He held this post till 1901. Sir Robert's special role in this world famous police body was Chief of the Criminal Investigation Department, the detectives' branch. Artist, Harry Furniss, in his book, *Some Victorian Men*, noted: 'One of the hardest-working and most brilliant heads of the Criminal Investigation Department for many years was that eminent Victorian, Sir Robert Anderson, KCB.'[2]

During his time at the Yard as 'super-sleuth', Sir Robert was in charge of many famous cases, including the 'Jack the Ripper' murders. The second of the 'ladies of the night' slayings happened the night before he took office. The destruction of two vital clues before the CID had a chance of viewing them and the unwillingness of a witness to give evidence were reasons in part for the murderer never being tried. Scotland Yard had no doubt as to the villain's identity: they believed he was an alien from Eastern Europe who probably died in an asylum.

Sir Robert's time at Scotland Yard did not go unrewarded. Queen Victoria in 1896 bestowed on him Companionship of the Order of the Bath and King Edward VII in 1901 conferred the honour of KCB, Knight Commander. During his retirement, Sir Robert continued his public-mindedness by writing and speaking extensively on prison reform.

Whilst Sir Robert carried out his public duties, he did not hide his deep faith. It was a moving spiritual experience shortly after his nineteenth birthday that led him to Jesus. One night he listened to an overseas speaker, Dr John Hall. Sir Robert sought to waylay Dr Hall and question him over his doctrine. His objections were cut short by the words: 'I tell you as a minister of Christ and in his name that there is life for you now if you will accept him. Will you accept Christ or reject him?' After a pause the thoughtful youth replied: 'In God's name, I will accept Christ.'

As a lawyer, secret service operative, leading civil servant and chief detective, Sir Robert had the necessary background and skills to investigate if Christ rose from the dead. Of the testimony of the witnesses to the resurrection as found in the Gospels he said that it 'would be accepted as valid by any fair tribunal in the world'. The resurrection 'is a public fact accredited by evidence which will stand the test of discussion and verification'.[3]

Sir Robert was a prolific writer. He authored seventeen Christian books, three secular books and numerous articles. His work, *Criminals and Crime* (1907), was a most insightful and bold treatise on prison reform. One of his best known articles is on Conan Doyle's fictional hero, entitled 'Sherlock Holmes as seen by Scotland Yard'.

Sir Robert's Christian writings earned an international readership. Dr Howard Mowll, former Anglican Archbishop of Sydney, wrote to Sir Robert's daughter that 'his books are still a great help to our theological students. . .' The *New York Tribune*'s reviewer of Sir Robert's *The Bible and Modern Criticism* decided that it 'is a work of singular lucidity of style and remarkable argumentative power which places [biblical] critics. . . on their defence before men of common sense'.[4] Some of his better known titles are: *A Doubter's Doubts About Science and Religion*, *The Coming Prince*, *The Lord From Heaven: A Study of the Deity of the Lord Jesus Christ*.[5]

Do the Gospel writers complement each other?

Sir Robert Anderson believes that the complementary character of the four Gospels is another indication that these writers are reliable witnesses. Let us look at two further tests of authenticity:

❏ The complementary test

I was involved in a case where two policemen, who were prosecution witnesses, lied. To support their claim, they invented a story about a motor vehicle they alleged was involved in the incident. The truth of the matter was this vehicle did not exist. In cross-examination their case was annihilated as they contradicted each other over the make, model and colour of the mystery car.

I was not surprised. When witnesses join together to fabricate a tale, inconsistencies are often found in their evidence. They tend to contradict each other in the detail. In their conspiracy, they fail to cover all possible contingencies and probing questions find them out. In contrast, truthful witnesses naturally complement each other.

When we closely examine the testimony of Matthew, Mark, Luke and John, we find that they complement each other. Consider these examples:

(a) *The Gospels record that Jesus came before the Sanhedrin Jewish ruling Council — in his last deathly hours.* The High Priest and other members of the Council were outraged as they believed Jesus had committed blasphemy. Matthew records the following drama: 'They spat in his face, and struck him; and some slapped him, saying, "Prophecy to us, you Christ! Who is it that struck you?".'

How could such a question be difficult? Why the need for supernatural prophecy? Matthew throws no light on the matter. But when we turn to Luke, the reason for the question becomes clear: 'when they had blindfolded him, they struck him. . .'[6]

(b) *There was an inscription placed on the cross of Christ.* Luke states it read, 'This is the King of the Jews', Mark, 'The King of the Jews', Matthew, 'This is Jesus the King of the Jews', and John, 'Jesus of Nazareth, the King of the Jews'.[7] The four writers complement each other in the general sense of the words used. Further, John notes that the sign was written in three different languages and thereby explains any difference in words used.

❏ The minor variations test
This test is not a contradiction of the above. Whilst truthful witnesses complement each other, a judge would not expect them to describe the same incidents in precisely the same way. If they did, that would point to conspiracy. Sometimes there may not be total uniformity in the order of events. One anticipates variations when two or more people testify about the same incident.

The Gospels are full of such minor variations:

(a) *The story of Barabbas*, the criminal released at the trial of Jesus, has variations. The apostles John and Matthew simply call him a notorious prisoner, whilst Mark and Luke lay stress on his being a murderer.[8]

(b) *The imprisonment of John the Baptist* was the result of his bold action in criticising King Herod's marriage to his brother's wife, according to Mark. Luke concurs, but takes the matter further and says John the Baptist had said other things that had also angered Herod.[9]

(c) *The healing of the leper* narrative varies slightly in Matthew, Mark and Luke. Matthew simply has the leper kneeling before Jesus, Mark has him not just on his knees, but pleading, and Luke states he was prostrate, face to the ground.[10]

Matthew, Mark, Luke and John pass these two further tests of reliability. Further, even if it could be established that the minor variations related not just to the style and emphasis of each writer, but included their understanding of what the facts were, this in itself would not mean their testimony would be disregarded. The court would ask whether such a discrepancy pertained to a fact of importance or just to a trivial detail before weighing its significance. Slight differences over trivia are not going to lead to the dismissing of the evidence as a whole.

A question in reply

It appears that, overall, the Gospel writers complement each other and their minor variations have the ring of truth about them. But is it not true that there are major discrepancies in their writings? Are there not discrepancies that some biblical critics make much of and which show up fatal flaws in the testimony?

When investigating the alleged Gospel discrepancies, as a lawyer I keep two legal terms in mind: harmonisation and cross examination:

❑ Harmonisation

Sir Norman Anderson, referred to in detail in chapter 6, has this to say about apparent major inconsistencies in the Gospels and in testimony in general:

> Is it not a matter of plain commonsense to make a reasonable attempt to resolve apparent inconsistencies in any web of evidence before jumping to the premature conclusion that the witnesses — or, indeed, one and the same witnesses — have presented us with 'glaring' and 'irreconcilable' contradiction?[11]

In other words, rather than becoming 'uptight'

over the inconsistencies, the proper approach is to actually seek to reconcile the alleged difficulties. Gleeson Archer, prominent biblical scholar and a law graduate, has this salutory word for those who avoid harmonisation:

> Bible critics who have never had any training in the laws of evidence may decry the 'harmonistic method' all they wish; but, like it or not, it is essentially the harmonistic method that is followed every day that court is in session throughout the civilised world. This method has a very definite bearing on valid procedures in biblical criticism as well as in the practical conduct of a tort or criminal action, or even a contract case in a court of law, today. Then the critics would find that most of their artificial, logically fallacious and basically biased approaches to the text of Holy Scripture would be successfully challenged by even the most inexperienced attorney and thrown out by the presiding judge.[12]

We shall now look at some alleged major inconsistencies and see if they can be naturally harmonised:

(a) *The siting of the Sermon on the Mount.* Matthew has the Sermon being delivered by Jesus as he sat on the mountain. On the other hand, Luke states: 'And [Jesus] came down with them and stood on a level place.'[13]

Harmonisation is natural and straightforward. The Sermon on the Mount is the longest discourse the Gospels record Jesus delivering. It is probable that Jesus delivered the Sermon sometimes sitting, sometimes standing on a plateau-like formation on the mountain. Historian and scholar, I. Howard

Marshall, states that 'a suitable site, halfway up the hillside, has been identified near Capernaum'.[14]

(b) *The resurrection of Jesus* account is found in all four Gospels. For years some biblical critics have suggested these stories contain major inconsistencies. John Wenham shows how the resurrection accounts are not in conflict.[15] The most detailed account of the empty tomb happenings is found in John. The other Gospels record part of what John states. While some have one angel and others two, there are simple explanations for this, one being there were different appearances; another, that one angel acted as spokesperson.

One particular resurrection account of interest is Luke chapter 24. Unlike John, Luke does not record any appearance of the risen Christ in Galilee. Luke chapter 24 need not be a continuous narrative and there could be a time break before the discourse that commences at verse 50. If that is so, there is sufficient time for the Galilean appearances. There was no obligation on Luke to schedule all of Jesus' resurrection appearances.

(c) *The healing narrative concerning the blind men outside Jericho* is recorded in three places and alleged major inconsistences between them cannot be easily harmonised.[16] The fact that Matthew mentions two blind men whereas Mark and Luke refer to one is not a problem in itself, because if there were two there was one. The problem arises in that Luke records the miracle as occurring whilst Jesus approached Jericho, but Matthew and Mark suggest that it took place as Jesus left Jericho. What are we to do?

Sir Robert Anderson comes to our assistance here

by giving a personal illustration with a legal application. He is speaking of a summer visit he made to an historic home in Ireland:

> The eldest son and daughter of the house left us one morning to spend the day with relatives some half-dozen miles away. Late at night, from my bedroom window, I saw the returning carriage drive up to the hall door. The lady alighted with a gentleman who was not her brother. At breakfast next morning she told us that her brother had remained at his cousins' house, and she had brought back a Mrs Somebody — mentioned a name I did not know. . . This enabled me to press the question whether a gentleman had not escorted her; and her answer was unequivocal that her only companion had been the lady she had named. When in my official life I have found conflict of testimony between persons of known integrity, I have always sought some way of reconciling them. But in this case I confess I was baffled. . . But I afterwards obtained from her the solution of the enigma. The lady she named was the wife of the doctor. His house was near the gate of the park (entrance to the historical home); and when his wife alighted he took her place in the carriage and drove with my friend to the hall door.[17]

The message here is that an apparent inconsistency in testimony may not be so when all the facts are known.

As we do not have all the facts behind the Gospel stories, and as the Gospel writers' accounts complement each other in so many instances, Sir Robert's wise counsel is that we should not dismiss the reliability of the Gospels simply because of one or two problem passages. A lawyer knows better and the solution to this apparent conflict may be as simple as the one Sir Robert has drawn from his own experience.

❑ Cross-examination

Many biblical critics are what we call 'negative higher critics'. 'Higher criticism' in itself is a useful tool and it asks questions about date, authorship, purpose, genre, background and how a book of the Bible became accepted by the community of faith. These are necessary considerations in scholarship.

However, 'negative higher critics' bring their own presumptions to the Bible. In many cases they have negated the supernatural in history, so miracles, prophecy and the like have to be explained away. These critics have a bias against special revelation and a reliable Bible preserved by the providence of God, and they *expect* to find problems in the Gospels. They hold there must always be long oral transmission of accounts originating from a variety of sources and situations. Consequently, there must be error and embellishment in due course. They will not let the Gospel documents speak for themselves, nor follow principles like harmonisation. Rather, their own presuppositions are primary.

The approach of the 'negative higher critics' receives little acceptance from lawyers. Their method should be critiqued, cross-examined. There are three questions lawyers would ask the critics:

(a) *Do they have the expertise to comment on the trustworthiness of the Gospels?* Are they truly expert witnesses? No. Unlike lawyers, these scholars on the whole have no tested background in determining what is a reliable document. Sir Robert Anderson indicates that whether or not there are damaging inconsistencies in the Gospels is a question of evidence and these critics' qualifications are not in this field.[18]

(b) *Have their findings been upheld in the past?* No. For example, one of the assertions of the early 'negative critics' was that there was no sophisticated writing amongst the Israelites before the time of the Monarchy, about 1000 BC. For this and other reasons it was held by Wellhausen and others that the first five books of the Old Testament must therefore have evolved over a long period of time through reliance on various oral traditions and sources, that the Pentateuch came together fairly late in Israel's history and it could not have originated from around the time of Moses.

Sir Robert states that now 'it is a matter of common knowledge that long before the time of Moses, literature flourished; and archaeological discovery tells us that in the century before the Exodus, Palestine was a land of books and schools'.[19]

(c) *Are they biased?* Yes. One's own world view must never override the facts. Yet the 'negative higher critics' are subject to their own presuppositions. Sir Norman Anderson states:

> Many of them, indeed, seem to accept or reject biblical evidence on what appears to be a purely subjective basis. They will not only quote, but also treat as authoritative and decisive, a passage which suits their thesis, yet they will completely ignore other passages which run counter to their argument. Again, they often appear to take singularly little trouble to interpret the document as

a whole and reject the elementary presumption that an author is intrinsically unlikely to have contradicted himself. Instead, they seem positively to swoop, on occasion, on contradictions which do not — or do not necessarily — in fact exist.[20]

My conclusion is that while it appears that Matthew, Mark, Luke and John contradict each other, the proper approach is to endeavour to harmonise these few incidents and, when we do, we find the testimony is complementary and solid.

Conclusion: the Pinocchio theory

How to know if a person is telling the truth? In the children's story of Pinocchio, Pinocchio's nose grew when he lied. Comically, his prominent facial feature was the measure of truthtelling.

In the case of Matthew, Mark, Luke and John, we do not have to rely on such a dubious method. There are legal tests for determining truth and in the last two chapters we have found that the Gospel writers pass those tests.

Endnotes:

1. A.P. Moore-Anderson, *Sir Robert Anderson and Lady Agnes Anderson*, Marshall, Morgan and Scott, 1947, p.15

2. Cited in *ibid*, p.49. For further insights into this man's career see Sir Robert Anderson's autobiography, *The Lighter Side of My Official Life*, Hodder and Stoughton, 1910

3. Sir Robert Anderson, *A Doubter's Doubts about Science and Religion*, 3rd ed., Pickering and Inglis, 1924, pp.96 and 101

4. Cited in A.P. Moore-Anderson, *op.cit.*, pp.87 and 138

5. Sir Robert Anderson, *A Doubter's Doubts about Scienceand Religion: The Coming Prince*, 19th ed., Kregel, 1975; and *The Lord from Heaven: A Study of the Deity of the Lord Jesus Christ*, 2nd ed., Kregel, 1978

6. Matthew 26, verses 67 and 68; Luke 22, verse 64

7. Luke 22, verse 38; Mark 15, verse 26; Matthew 27, verse 37; John 19, verses 19 and 20

8. Matthew 28, verses 15 to 26; Mark 15, verses 1 to 15; Luke 23, verses 1 to 25; John 18, verses 28 to 40

9. Mark 6, verses 14 to 29; Luke 3, verses 19 and 20

10. Matthew 8, verses 1 to 4; Mark 1, verses 40 to 45; Luke 5, verses 12 to 16

11. Norman Anderson, *A Lawyer among the Theologians*, Hodder and Stoughton, 1973, p.111

12. Gleason C. Archer, *Encyclopedia of Bible Difficulties*, Zondervan, 1982, p.315

13. Matthew 5, verse 1; Luke 6, verse 17

14. I. Howard Marshall, *The Gospel of Luke*, The New International Greek Testament Commentary, Paternoster, 1978, p.241

15. John Wenham, *Easter Enigma*, Zondervan, 1984

16. Matthew 20, verses 29 to 34; Mark 10, verses 46 to 52; Luke 18, verses 35 to 45

17. Sir Robert Anderson, *The Bible and Modern Criticism*, 5th ed., Hodder and Stoughton, 1905, pp.221-222

18. Sir Robert Anderson, *A Doubter's Doubt about Science and Religion*, pp.154-155

19. *Ibid*, p.148

20. Norman Anderson, *op.cit.*, p.20

5

Lord Hailsham:
The former Lord Chancellor

*Is the Jesus story found outside
the New Testament?*

LORD HAILSHAM WAS BORN Quintin McGarel Hogg.
After private tuition, Eton and a classics degree at
Oxford University, where he obtained a double
First in 1930, he trained in law. This educational
background was the foundation for an outstanding
career in law and politics.

His political career began in 1938 when, as Quintin Hogg, he was elected to the House of Commons.
Lord Hailsham was prominent in the British parliament and 'along with Lord Hinchingbrooke and
Lord Thorneycroft, he was instrumental in having
the Beveridge Report — which laid the foundation
of the Welfare State — accepted in principle by the
Conservative leaders'.[1]

From 1956 until 1964 he held diverse political offices, such as First Lord of the Admiralty, Minister
of Education, Minister for Science and Technology,

and Minister with Special Responsibility for Sport.

The legal achievements of Lord Hailsham are just as noteworthy. In 1953 he became a Queen's Counsel, a special honour bestowed on an outstanding barrister. He then served two periods as Lord High Chancellor, the pre-eminent English judicial officer. In consequence, he was created a life peer, taking the title Baron Hailsham of St Marylebone — he had given up his hereditary peerage previously. Amongst other roles, the Lord Chancellor acts as Speaker of the House of Lords and is a member of the Privy Council and of the Cabinet.

His private life has been tinged with sadness. Lord Hailsham's mother died when he was seventeen of an unexpected stroke. In 1978 his wife, who accompanied him to Australia for the Inaugural Sir Robert Menzies Oration, was killed in a horse-riding accident in Centennial Park, Sydney. His eldest brother, who was an author, lawyer and Member of Parliament, committed suicide.

Lord Hailsham's spiritual journey cannot be separated from his life experiences. His parents, though not overtly religious, taught him the rudiments: the Lord's Prayer, the Apostle's Creed, how to say grace and prayers, what the Bible is all about. He was baptised and confirmed in the Anglican Church, but all this made little impression. The death of his mother undermined any religious convictions he might have had, although he did not openly cut his ties with the church.

A spiritual abyss, however, was not to be a permanent state for Lord Hailsham. At twenty-three whilst doing a logic paper at Oxford University, he surprisingly found himself reassessing his position. He started again to attend church. He recommenced praying and, as time passed, he committed himself to theism and then Jesus Christ.

Lord Hailsham suggests two main factors were responsible for his renewed Christian belief. The first was a growing conviction about Christ as the One who died and rose again. This became the cornerstone of his faith: 'Were either [Jesus's death and resurrection] proved not to have happened in any sense, the church ought to disappear and, I think, it would do so'.[2] The second was his growing appreciation of the role of the living church:

> How much of what is now taken for granted in what is good in society owes its original inspiration to a consciously Christian motivation. . . Our whole system of education, public and private, our network of hospitals, our social security system itself, have each a clear origin in Christian foundations. . . The Christians have been pioneers of good works throughout their history. They have been the originators and secular society has largely caught up with their efforts, made good their deficiencies of scale and corrected their faults.[3]

Lord Hailsham is arguably the most influential legal figure and political philosopher in recent British history and much may be learned from him.

His writings are many and varied and include *The Dilemma of Democracy*. It is his autobiography, *The Door Wherein I Went*, which tells much about this man and his spiritual pilgrimage.[4] In it, Lord Hailsham includes a brief discussion of the evidence for Jesus in the pages of secular history. Lord

Hailsham's Jesus, though, is more than a revered historical figure as he brings strength and hope to the sufferings of life:

> I once did a case in which my function was to defend a young mother who had beaten her little daughter, aged two or three, to death... And I read in the evidence, happily among the statements not given in court, how the little being just before she died, said the heart-breaking words: 'I'm sorry, Mummy...'
>
> How can a good God permit such dreadful things to happen, I ask myself helplessly... The one thing which keeps me sane and well-balanced in such moods of black despair is the memory of Christ's passion, his shameful conviction, his cruel mishandling, his slow death and the ultimate hopelessness of his cry of dereliction... a statement that God the invisible — the Creator, the ground of all being, without body, parts or passions — enters into human suffering with us and somehow agonises in all our private Gethsemanes.[5]

Is the Jesus story found outside the New Testament?

Lord Hailsham makes this comment:

> Communists teach that there was no such person as Jesus at all. He was a Sun myth, like Mithras, or perhaps a rain god like Quezalcoatl. He is the unperson to end all unpeople. It might be possible to ignore this view as too absurd to be taken seriously were it not for the fact that so many people must be growing up to believe just this.[6]

The communist, however, is not alone in his rejection of an historical Jesus and the tragedy is that such a dismissal is contrary to all the evidence before us. We have already discovered the trustworthiness of the Gospel testimony. Let me now document some of the evidence for Jesus outside of the New Testament that is available to any enquirer.

❏ Jewish sources

(a) *Flavius Josephus* began life in Jerusalem in about AD 37. He was an educated man who commanded Jewish forces in the rebellion against Rome. After defeat, he became a friend of the Roman Emperor.

He devoted the second half of his life to writing books on the history of Jews. He said this of Jesus:

> Now, there was about this time Jesus, a wise man if it be lawful to call him a man, for he was a doer of wonderful works — a teacher of such men as receive the truth with pleasure. He drew over to him both many of the Jews and many of the Gentiles. He was [the] Christ; and when Pilate, at the suggestion of the principal men amongst us, had condemned him to the cross, those that loved him at the first did not forsake him, for he appeared to them alive again the third day, as the divine prophets had foretold these and ten thousand other wonderful things concerning him; and the tribe of Christians, so named from him, are not extinct at this day.[7]

Some people seek to dismiss this Josephus reference on the grounds that it appears to go considerably further in its affirmations about Christ than one would expect from a non-Christian. They claim it has been subject to Christian editing.

My answer to this objection is fourfold:

* This statement has as good manuscript evidence as anything in Josephus.
* Legally, the burden of proof lies with those who doubt the authenticity of Josephus' statement to produce concrete evidence in rebuttal.
* The statement on the whole is accepted by classical scholars. The late E.M. Blaiklock, former Professor of Classics at the University of Auckland, New Zealand, states:

> I must confess that I myself, until recently, dismissed the [Josephus] passage as of doubtful authenticity and as unreliable evidence in New Testament apologetics. I discovered that colleagues in classical history had passed me by and recognised a depository of genuine information. They led me to re-examine the whole position.[8]

* An Arabian manuscript of the passage has been found and it was released in 1972 by Professor Schlomo Pines of the Hebrew University in Jerusalem. It notes all the same facts about Jesus, but does so minus the affirmations that suggest Josephus personally accepted all that was said. So clearly, whether one accepts the Josephus statement verbatim, there is no doubt he did chronicle the fact that Jesus lived and died and it was believed he performed miracles and rose again.

Josephus also mentions other New Testament characters. He speaks of the baptisms of John the Baptist and documents the execution of this John, as well as James, the brother of Jesus.

(b) *Jewish literature.* The Jewish Talmud[9] notes Jesus' execution, that he was not accepted by Jewish authorities, that he hung on a tree on Passover eve and that he did 'miracles'.

The Jewish sources are clearly the best external evidence, as it is unlikely they are based on hearsay or Christian propaganda. They are an independent record.

❑ Pagan literature

(a) *Pliny the Younger* was sent to Bithynia to reorganise the affairs of the province and in about AD 110 he wrote a letter to Emperor Trajan. He confirmed his persecution of Christians and gave a portrait of the early Christian community as worshippers of Christ who sang to him as God.[10]

(b) *Cornelius Tacitus*, a Roman historian, in AD 112, stated Jesus was put to death by Pontius Pilate during the reign of Tiberius.[11] In the same paragraph he records that Nero tried to blame the Christians for his famous fire of AD 64 and that he tortured them relentlessly.

(c) *Suetonius*, the official historian of the Imperial house, in AD 120 described the expelling of the Jews from Rome and their allegiance to Chrestus. 'Chrestus' is an accepted ancient variation of 'Christus', Latin for Christ.[12]

From the Jewish and pagan sources I have listed, we learn the following facts about Jesus:

* he had a brother, James;
* he was called the Christ (Messiah);
* he was known to be a teacher;
* he was a doer of miracles;

* he had followers;
* he was not popular with the Jewish religious leaders;
* Pontius Pilate put him to death and this happened on a Passover during the reign of Tiberius Caesar (AD 14–37);
* many believed he rose from the dead;
* Christianity spread quickly to Rome and often persecution followed.

It is important to note that the above points are consistent with what the evangelists — Matthew, Mark, Luke and John — tell us about the Christ event. The external accounts of Christ confirm the Gospel story.

❏ Other so-called 'Christian' sources

(a) *The Gnostic Gospels.* Some people have told me that they place great significance on a cache of thirteen Coptic codices which was discovered in 1946 near Nag Hammadi, Upper Egypt. The cache was deposited in about AD 400 and it contains some forty-three treatises, the best known of which is the Gospel according to Thomas. This quasi-Gnostic Gospel contains 114 sayings attributed to Jesus.

The Gnostic Gospels are the reflections of religious movements that taught that salvation comes through a secret 'gnosis' or knowledge, and that the material creation, including our fleshly body, is evil — teachings inconsistent with those of Christ.

The Gnostic writings, however, from Nag Hammadi and elsewhere, add little to our understanding of the Jesus of history. They have no substantial internal or external evidence that supports that they were written by eyewitnesses to the Christ event and are therefore not primary source material. Further, they do not have the status of reliable, historical books. In fact, many Gnostic writings are put out in the name of a famous person of a previous era, thus giving the new work a quick acceptance.

The Gnostic teachings are often inconsistent with those of the New Testament Gospel writers whom we know were close to Christ. For example, in the Gospel of Thomas, Peter argues: 'Let Mary (probably Mary Magdalene) go away from among us because women are not worthy of the Life.' Jesus responds: 'See, I shall lead her, so that I will make her male that she too may become a living spirit, resembling you males. For every woman who makes herself a male will enter the Kingdom of Heaven.' Such an aversion to womanhood is contrary to the outlook of Christ as seen in Matthew, Mark, Luke and John.

(b) *Apocryphal New Testament.* This collection of writings was rejected by the followers of Christ, again for the books' inconsistency and speculative nature. Much of it endeavours to fill in the gaps — it gives us personal details about Christ and other characters that is not found in the Gospels. For example, the Gospel of Bartholomew talks about what Jesus did between his death and resurrection, whilst the Gospel of Peter focuses on the actual resurrection.

Dr J.B. Phillips, eminent scholar and translator of the New Testament into modern English, has a pertinent comment:

Probably most people have not had the opportunity to read the apocryphal 'gospels' and 'epistles', although every scholar has. I can only say here that in such writings we live in a world of magic and make-believe, of myth and fancy. In the whole task of translating the New Testament, I never for one moment, however provoked and challenged I might be, felt that I was being swept away into a world of spookiness, witchcraft and magical powers such as abound in the books rejected from the New Testament. It was the sustained down-to-earth faith of the New Testament writers which conveyed to me that inexpressible sense of the genuine and the authentic.[13]

The Gnostic Gospels and Apocryphal New Testament are in vogue in certain academic circles. They are certainly entertaining and interesting to read, but offer little in one's honest search for historical information about Christ. They do not pass the legal tests. We should rely on the Jewish and pagan sources and the New Testament.

A question in reply

We have found there is non-biblical evidence for Christ, but is it not meagre? It is a good point, but it should not surprise us. Jesus had a life of humble beginnings, died an early death and led no political revolution. Ancient reporters tended to cover the events surrounding well-to-do people.

In fact, Jesus must have made some impact to receive the 'press' he did. Of course, as the risen Christ continued to influence people, his story then became the centre of history. However, the early sources are important and do show that Jesus was an historical person.

There is another point to note here. We have already seen that the Gospels are reliable, historical documents and primary source material. The fact that at a later time they were included in the Christian New Testament does not alter this situation. So history is far from silent on Christ.

Lord Hailsham's words are a fitting conclusion to this chapter:

The Christians were perfectly well-known in the reign of Trajan and at least as early as the reign of Nero. Pliny writes about them from Bythinia. . . It is wholly inconceivable that if their founder about sixty or seventy years before Trajan had never existed or never been crucified, someone — Greek, Roman or Jew — would not have said so. One might as well cast doubt on the existence of General Booth [Founder of the Salvation Army, 1829–1912].[14]

Endnotes:

1. The legal Inner Temple magazine *Pegasus*, 5, 1984, cited in *The Simon Greenleaf Law Review*, IV, 1984–1985, p.x
2. Lord Hailsham, *The Door Wherein I Went*, Collins, 1975, pp. 46-47
3. *Ibid*, p.48
4. *Ibid*
5. *Ibid*, pp.40-41
6. *Ibid*, p.28
7. Flavius Josephus, *Antiquities* XVIII 3.3
8. E.M. Blaiklock, *Jesus Christ: Man or Myth*, Nelson, 1984, pp.29-30
9. See, for example, Sanhedrin 43a and Yeb.IV 3:49a
10. Pliny the Younger, *Epistles* X 96
11. Cornelius Tacitus, *Annals* XV 44.2-8
12. Suetonius, *Life of Claudius*, 25.4
13. J.B. Phillips, *The Ring of Truth*, rpt, Marshall, Morgan and Scott, 1984, p.123
14. Lord Hailsham, *op.cit.*, p.29

6

Sir Norman Anderson:
An eminent law professor

What is the real evidence for the resurrection?

'I HAVE CERTAINLY HAD a more variegated and interesting life than I had ever expected,' Sir Norman Anderson has said.

He was born in Suffolk, England in 1908. His childhood was a lonely one, mainly due to the fact that his sisters were much older and a brother died in infancy. He was educated at a small public school and then read Law at Cambridge University. He commenced his legal studies as a committed Christian:

> Some children of Christian parents seem to grow imperceptibly into a knowledge of God as their Father and Jesus as their Saviour. It was somewhat like this — but in a very faltering way — with me. I heard the gospel when I was very young and I cannot remember a time when I did not try to respond. But my faith was painfully weak, and I went through the process of confession of sin and self-commitment to Christ again and again; it was

not until I was about fifteen that I came to what is commonly called 'assurance'.[1]

This teenage commitment did not diminish, even though there was personal tragedy. Sir Norman's son Hugh, who was the leader of the Labour movement at Cambridge University, died aged twenty-two. Within five years of Hugh's death, Sir Norman lost his two daughters.

The influence of Sir Norman has crossed national borders. He is a respected legal figure in England, United States, British Commonwealth countries and the Middle East and has been a visiting lecturer at Princeton University, New York University and the Harvard Law School. He was offered a professorship for life at Harvard.

His reputation is not confined to the law. He is a leading layman in the Anglican Church, having been Lay Chairman of the General Synod of the Church of England. He is an internationally renowned author and lecturer on topics ranging from ethics to comparative religion. He has also received many military and civil honours, including a knighthood in 1975.[2]

The University of London has been a large part of Sir Norman's academic life. Before his retirement, he held such strategic offices as: Professor of Oriental Laws; Head of the Department of Law, School of Oriental and African Studies; Dean of the Faculty of Laws; and Director of the Institute of Advanced Legal Studies. Upon his retirement, Sir Norman became an honorary member of Cambridge University Law Faculty.

Sir Norman's career, however, has not been confined to English universities. He has a more adventurous spirit. He was a missionary in Egypt from 1931 to 1940. Whilst there, he faced the challenge of World War II and served in part as Arab Liaison Officer, Libyan Arab Force, and was later absorbed into the Occupied Enemy Territories Administration. In wartime he served with distinction and rose to the rank of colonel.

It is not surprising when one considers Sir Norman's legal, missionary and war background that he came to specialise in Islamic law. He has written and lectured extensively on this subject and was awarded a doctorate of laws from Cambridge University on the strength of his work in this field.

Sir Norman has written some eighteen books in all, including a 250,000 word tome, *Islamic Law in Africa*. Most of his works have focused on religion and Christianity. He wrote his first Christian book in Arabic.

The motivation for Sir Norman's writing on the Christian faith is to 'share with others the greatest story in the world (together with some of its implications) as understood by a lawyer who sees it not only as deeply satisfying but essentially reasonable'.[3] This story, for him, is about the person of Jesus:

> He was unique: in all he did, in all he said, in all he was. Whatever way we look at him, he is in a class by himself. Even apart from the resurrection, there are excellent and convincing reasons for believing that he was 'God manifest in the flesh'.
>
> Why then is it incredible that such a one rose from the dead? It would have been far more incredible if he had not.[4]

His books include: *Jesus Christ: The Witness of History*, *Christianity and World Religions: The Challenge of Pluralism*, *A Lawyer among the Theologians*, *The Teaching of Jesus* and *The Evidence for the Resurrection.*[5]

What is the real evidence for the resurrection?

The resurrection, the key to the Christian faith, is the focus of Sir Norman's writings. He argues that if Jesus arose, his claims to be Lord, God and Saviour must be taken seriously. If he lies in the grave, he is only one amongst many gurus.

He argues that this view of the resurrection was central to the apostles:

> Both the deity of Jesus and the efficacy of his atoning death were. . . proved for the apostles by the fact of his resurrection. From the first, the confident assertion that Jesus had been raised from death was the basis and starting-point of their proclamation.[6]

As no eyewitness was present in the tomb the moment Jesus rose from the dead, the legal evidence required to prove his resurrection is twofold. Firstly, one must prove that Jesus Christ was dead — beyond resuscitation — at point A. Secondly, it must be shown that he was alive at point B. There is no need to establish what caused the resurrection. If someone is dead then alive, the only reasonable inference is resurrection!

I will now set out a legal case for the resurrection of Jesus. We will consider what the four Gospels say, remembering it has been established that they are reliable, historical documents written by people close to Christ who were committed to telling the truth. However, we will not limit ourselves to the Gospels and we will call further evidence where appropriate.

1. Was Jesus dead at point A?

❏ Was his trial fair?

The Gospels record six inquisitions.[7] The following events took place in the twelve hours from the time of Jesus' arrest in the Garden of Gethsemane around midnight Thursday until his crucifixion at noon on Friday:

* Jesus came before Annas, former Jewish High Priest.
* Jesus came before Caiaphas, High Priest.
* Jesus came before the Sanhedrin, the Jewish Council that had religious and certain civil and criminal jurisdiction over the Jews.
* Jesus came before Pilate, the Roman Governor.
* Jesus came before Herod, King of Galilee, a Roman appointee.
* Jesus came before Pilate again.

In summary, there were six inquisitions and two parts to Jesus' trial: the Jewish and the Roman hearings.

Many lawyers believe Jesus was denied basic civil and legal rights. An American lawyer, David K. Breed, has found seventeen errors and injustices that took place in the trials of Christ. Some of them are:

* No *legal* process could take place on the Jewish Sabbath or on feast days. (At the time of Jesus' trial, the Jews were observing the Passover.)

* No *legal* process could be started at night for a trial before a regular Sanhedrin court.
* The courts erred by not taking into consideration the guilt or innocence of Jesus.
* Pilate, having announced Jesus not guilty, erred in permitting the verdict of the 'mob' to stand. The record shows Christ, after Pilate found 'no harm' in him, was sent to Herod, then back to Pilate, then turned over to be crucified.
* It was unlawful and therefore an error for the Sanhedrin to convict on the same day as the trial; they could acquit the same day, but had to hold a verdict of 'guilty' under advisement at least two days.[8]

Sir Leslie Herron, former Chief Justice of New South Wales, Australia, agrees that there were great injustices in the trials. He holds that the evidence indicates that the Jewish preferred course was secretly to murder Jesus, but at the last moment they were forced into a public hearing.[9]

The eventual Jewish charge was blasphemy. Certainly Caiaphas held Jesus had committed blasphemy and this was confirmed in his mind by Jesus' admission that he claimed to be the 'Son of God' and 'Son of Man'.[10]

Some have argued that these titles do not in themselves constitute blasphemy as the terms do not necessarily imply Jesus was claiming to be divine. However, such an approach fails to take cognisance of what Jesus meant by these words. For example, in Mark chapter 2, Jesus forgave sins and said the Son of Man had authority to do so.

The Jewish teachers were angry because they knew that by such action Jesus was taking the prerogative of and claiming equality with the Almighty.

Jesus was properly charged, even though the trials were in many ways a farce. He did claim equality with God, a chargeable offence, as Simon Greenleaf states:

> For whether the accusations were founded on the first or second commands in the [Ten Commandments] or on the law, laid down in the thirteenth chapter of Deuteronomy, or on that in the eighteenth chapter and twentieth verse, he had violated them all, by assuming to himself powers belonging alone to Jehovah.[11]

The Jewish leaders sentenced Christ to death. The verdict itself was a travesty of justice because Jesus was truly God as the resurrection would verify. The Sanhedrin could not alone carry out the death penalty, so they took Jesus to Pontius Pilate. Pilate no doubt viewed Jesus more as a political rather than religious criminal, but acquiesced in agreeing to the death penalty.

❏ Was the death sentence carried out?
Yes, of this fact there is no doubt. The evidence is as follows:

● Direct evidence
(a) *John, Peter and Matthew.* John records the execution of Jesus by a cross and Roman spear and confirms he was a witness to it. He stresses he actually saw it and therefore knows it happened:

Later, knowing that all was now completed and so that the Scripture would be fulfilled, Jesus said, 'I am thirsty.' A jar of wine vinegar was there, so they soaked a sponge in it, put the sponge on a stalk of the hyssop plant and lifted it to Jesus' lips. When he had received the drink, Jesus said, 'It is finished.' With that he bowed his head and gave up his spirit.

Now it was the day of Preparation and the next day was to be a special Sabbath. Because the Jews did not want the bodies left on the crosses during the Sabbath, they asked Pilate to have the legs broken and the bodies taken down. The soldiers therefore came and broke the legs of the first man who had been crucified with Jesus, and then those of the other. But when they came to Jesus and found that he was already dead, they did not break his legs. Instead, one of the soldiers pierced Jesus' side with a spear, bringing a sudden flow of blood and water. The man who saw it has given testimony and his testimony is true. He knows that he tells the truth and he testifies so that you also may believe.[12]

The evidence also points to Peter being there. He was present at some of the inquisitions of Jesus and was not amongst the disciples who fled after Jesus' arrest.[13] Peter's account is found in Mark and asserts Jesus was crucified until dead.[14]

Matthew chronicles the death of Christ and, although he hid after they arrested Jesus, he returned by the time of the execution.[15] Those who have any doubt about the presence of John, Peter and Matthew at the death of Jesus should listen to the words of historian Luke:

But *all* those who knew him, including the women who had followed him from Galilee, stood at a distance watching these things.[16]

(b) *The women.* The Gospels record that a number of women observed the execution of Jesus. Matthew mentions Mary Magdalene, Mary the mother of James and Joseph and Zebedee's wife, the mother of John. At least two of these women witnessed the actual burial of Jesus.[17]

(c) *Joseph of Arimathea and Nicodemus.* These two Jewish leaders, members of the Sanhedrin, took the dead body of Jesus away and buried him. They knew what Jesus looked like and could not be mistaken as to whose body they had.[18] As the burial was performed by men who were not actual public followers of Jesus, there is no possibility here of conspiracy or of Jesus faking his death.

● **Other documentary evidence**
As we have seen in the previous chapter, there are non-Christian reports by Roman and Jewish historians that acknowledge the death of Jesus by crucifixion. These could be considered by a court. In particular, there is the evidence of the Roman Cornelius Tacitus who states that Jesus was put to death by Pontius Pilate during the reign of Tiberius.

And then there is the report of Jewish historian, Josephus, who affirms the death of Jesus.

❏ **What was the cause of death?**
The unlawful execution caused Jesus' death. This involved Jesus being flogged, struck on the face with a staff and being nailed to a cross. On the cross one died of suffocation, if not heart failure.

In Jesus' case there was also a spear thrust into his side. It must have been a savage thrust as it produced a deep wound, evidenced by the fact that Thomas could later place his hand in Jesus' side and John was aware of the flow of blood and water it produced.

I understand that such a flow of blood and water after death would only take place if the spear pierced a major artery or the heart itself.[19] The spear in the side of Jesus had been predicted in the Old Testament[20] and the shedding of blood is consistent with the Jewish sacrifice for forgiveness of sins. The death took place in or about April AD 33. This date fits the Gospel and other historical reports.

The Qu'ran denies the crucifixion of Jesus and claims he was taken up to heaven alive (Surah 4:156-159). In response, it should be stated the Qu'ran account is not based on any direct or documentary evidence.

❏ **Finding**
In or about April AD 33, Jesus of Nazareth was executed by Roman authorities upon a cross at Golgotha near Jerusalem. These are the material facts. Jesus died at point A.

2. Was Jesus alive at point B?
● **Direct testimony**
(a) *John, Peter and Matthew.* John has much to testify about. He went to the tomb and found it empty, and was also present at an encounter Jesus had with the disciples on the Sunday after his death.[21] He was there when the doubts of Thomas were swept aside:

Now Thomas (called Didymus), one of the Twelve, was not with the disciples when Jesus came. So the other disciples told him, 'We have seen the Lord!' But he said to them, 'Unless I see the nail marks in his hands and put my finger where the nails were, and put my hand into his side, I will not believe it.'

A week later his disciples were in the house again, and Thomas was with them. Though the doors were locked, Jesus came and stood among them and said, 'Peace be with you!'

Then he said to Thomas, 'Put your finger here; see my hands. Reach out your hand and put it into my side. Stop doubting and believe.' Thomas said to him, 'My Lord and my God!' Then Jesus told him, 'Because you have seen me, you have believed; blessed are those who have not seen and yet have believed.'[22]

The apostle John had a further moving meeting with Jesus whilst fishing with a small group by the Sea of Galilee. John had no doubts about what he saw.[23]

Matthew testifies that he was in the presence of Jesus after his death. He says the disciples and Jesus gathered together on a mountain in Galilee. There they worshipped him and received their final instructions:

Then Jesus came to them and said, 'All authority in heaven and on earth has been given to me. Therefore go and make disciples of all nations, baptising them in the name of the Father and of the Son and of the Holy Spirit, and teaching them to obey everything I have commanded you. And surely I am with you always, to the very end of the age.'[24]

The apostle Peter in the testimony he is primarily responsible for, Mark's Gospel, also testifies to meeting Jesus after his death.[25] There is debate as to whether verses 9 to 20 of chapter 16 are authentic as some of the old manuscripts conclude at verse 8. This need not concern us, because much of what Peter says here is reported in the other Gospels and certainly John and Matthew vouch that Peter witnessed the resurrection appearances.[26] Peter's other writings, his epistles, also indicate that Peter could testify about Jesus being alive after his death.[27]

As in the section that dealt with the death of Jesus, I have initially recorded what John, Matthew and Peter witnessed and wrote. Legally this is the best evidence, as they wrote about their own personal experiences. Paul also documents his own observations on the risen Christ.

(b) *Other disciples*. Apart from what John, Matthew and Peter describe from their own experience, they indicate, along with historian Luke, that the other eight disciples saw Jesus alive after his death. Twice the disciples met with Jesus in a room in Jerusalem. They were with him on a mountain. Luke states that the disciples even ate fish with the risen Christ, proving he was physically resurrected.[28]

These eight disciples corroborate the testimony of John, Matthew and Peter.

(c) *Mary Magdalene*. She was the first person to see the risen Christ. There is an ancient tradition that this Mary is the prostitute referred to in Luke 7, verses 36 to 50 – the woman who kissed Jesus' feet and poured ointment over them. John implies she is the sister of Lazarus, the man whom Jesus raised from the dead.[29] Mary, we are told, met Jesus near the tomb. When she realised it was Jesus, she cried out in Aramaic, 'Rabboni. . .', teacher. Mary touched the risen Christ and then went off to the disciples with the news, 'I have seen the Lord.'[30]

(d) *The other Mary.* Mary was the mother of James, an apostle of Christ. She saw Jesus alive after his death and touched his body. Other women were present, but only she and Mary Magdalene are mentioned by name.[31]

It is important to note the quality of these two women's testimony. They both saw the execution and burial of Christ. They give an unbroken chain of testimony from his death at point A to resurrection at point B. They were certain he died and rose again.[32] They were not considered reliable witnesses in that culture. If the Gospel writers were inventing this part of the story, they would have ensured that men provided the important unbroken chain of testimony.[33]

(e) *Two followers of Christ.* These men are not members of the twelve and they spent time with the risen Jesus on the road to Emmaus. This testimony in Luke chapter 24 is one of the most vivid of the resurrection narratives. It is so personal that many feel it indicates Luke is the unnamed disciple in the account.

(f) *Anyone in the crowd of 500.* The apostle Paul documents that such a crowd saw Jesus alive after his death.[34] This incident probably took place on the hills of Galilee some three or four weeks after the resurrection of Christ. Paul highlights that many of these witnesses were still alive and, by so doing, he was challenging the reader to verify this for himself.

Sir Norman makes the following comments on Paul's account:

> Paul was no fool, and he knew perfectly well that he had a host of enemies eager to pounce on him if he made a questionable statement. So it is exceedingly unlikely that he would have staked his whole credibility on the fact that there were three or four hundred persons still alive who claimed to have seen the risen Christ if this had not been the simple truth. It was tantamount to saying: 'If you don't believe me, there are plenty of people who can confirm this statement. Go and ask them.'[35]

(g) *James, earthly brother of Jesus.* He saw Jesus alive after his death.[36] James went on to be a leader of the early church.

(h) *The apostle Paul.* He encountered the risen Christ.[37] Paul was the arch enemy of the early church — he zealously persecuted the first followers. The meeting with Jesus transformed him from leading sceptic to a devoted disciple. His testimony is of the character of Matthew, Peter and John as he records his own experience.[38]

Lord Lyttleton (1709–1773), English politician and Chancellor of the Exchequer, stated:

> Besides all the proofs of [Christianity] which may be drawn from the prophecies of the Old Testament, from the necessary connexion it has with the whole system of the Jewish religion, from the miracles of Christ and from the evidence given of his resurrection by all the apostles, I thought the conversion and the apostleship of St Paul alone,

duly considered, was of itself a demonstration sufficient to prove Christianity to be a divine revelation.[39]

The above is a list of witnesses called to give direct testimony and, whilst they have all long since died, their observations are reliably documented for us. It is the type of evidence one can base a decision on. Lawyers, judges and juries would find it a strong parade of witnesses. Nevertheless, there are problems that should be addressed:

PROBLEM 1: *Can we really rely on these witnesses who were Jesus' friends? Would it not be a stronger case if the witnesses were strangers?*

Let me address this perceived problem:

* Not all the eyewitnesses were necessarily friends of Jesus. Some of the 500 who saw the risen Christ may well have been sceptics.
* James was not initially a follower of Jesus. John honestly narrates that Jesus' brothers did not believe in Jesus.[40] No doubt it was seeing Jesus alive after his death that transformed James.
* Paul began as one openly hostile to Jesus.[41]
* In the previous chapters it has been shown that Matthew, Mark, Luke and John were truthful men following a man of integrity. They were not fabricators. They really believed that the resurrection appearances which they record occurred.
* Apart from the above considerations, the truth of the matter is that eyewitnesses do make mistakes. However, when the witness previously knew the subject, that enhances the identification.

As one authority asserts, 'In an eyewitness context, the greatest challenge to the advocate's power of persuasion is presented by the attempt to argue, without support from expert testimony, the unreliability of an unimpeached eyewitness 'identification' of a prior acquaintance. . .'[42]

So the fact that some of the eyewitnesses who identified Jesus as being alive were friends of his is not a problem. It guarantees we have the right man. The one who died on the cross is definitely the one later seen alive. God has preserved for us the best eyewitness identification possible.

* There was good reason for Jesus being selective in his appearances.[43] The religious and civil authorities and others had already rejected his previous miracles and put him to death. Many for various reasons were threatened by his claims. Jesus clearly was not seeking another hostile confrontation and he had already said and done enough for people to place their faith in him. Irrespective of what testimony one would like, the direct eyewitness testimony we have is more than sufficient to establish Jesus' defeat of the grave.

PROBLEM 2: *Could the eyewitnesses have been subject to hallucination or some other pathological or physical phenomenon that sometimes follows the severe depression that accompanies the death of a friend? Could this not explain the testimony of Jesus being alive? They believed they saw him, but. . .!*

Sir Norman dismisses this objection. As a lawyer he knows it would not stand up and his findings can be summarised as follows:

* Only certain types of people are normally subject to such experiences. The witnesses of the resurrection appearances included people with a wide variety of backgrounds and dispositions.
* Hallucinations are highly individualistic, as their source is the subconscious mind and no two people will undergo exactly the same phenomena. The Gospel documents proclaim similar encounters for many people.
* Such phenomena usually are a result of one's long-term wish for a desired event. The New Testament indicates the disciples were sad and dejected; they were not expecting anything.
* Psychic experiences usually occur at suitable times and places. These 'hallucinations' occurred at many different times, including during an afternoon walk.
* Such happenings usually repeat themselves over a long time. By contrast, the appearances of Christ stopped after a short period of forty days.[44]

● Circumstantial evidence

In law, this is not evidence of the fact at issue — in our case Jesus being alive at point B — but is evidence supporting other facts that lead one to this conclusion.

For example, in a murder case, direct evidence is the testimony of someone who saw who fired the shot. Circumstantial evidence would include that the accused had purchased the rifle found at the scene, his fingerprints were on it and the deadly bullet matched other bullets fired from the rifle. The role of the lawyer is to build a strong chain of circumstantial evidence from which the court can deduce what took place.

Here is some of the circumstantial evidence that supports Jesus being alive at point B. This is evidence a court of law today would be called to consider. Such information as this can be found in the writings of Sir Norman and other lawyers:

(a) *History indicates the tomb of Christ was not subject to early pilgrimages.* This implies that his first followers did not believe he was still dead. One can compare this to the pilgrimages to Lenin's tomb.

(b) *There is the existence of the church itself.* It can be traced back to about AD 33 and its origins are based on the resurrection of its founder. If Christ had not risen, the New Testament indicates that there would have been no reason for the church existing.[45] Paul and the others were not interested in just another guru and religion.

(c) *Christians worship on Sunday and not the day of the Jewish sabbath.* The Jews were bound to their traditions and laws and, since the early Christians were Jewish, it must have taken an event of deep significance to cause them to change their day of worship. The resurrection happened on a Sunday. The Christians see each succeeding Sunday as a commemoration of this event.

(d) *There is the change that the living Christ has produced in people's lives.* Transformed and strengthened lives are circumstantial evidence that the Christian faith is strong. Examples can be produced from the time of the disciples to the present. An unbroken chain of testimony of changed lives leads to Jesus as the source. We can find the stories of enriched lives in autobiographies, the New Testament, in history and within the pages of this book.

Let's take, for example, the testimony of Australian, John Robilliard. John was born with a congenital heart abnormality. He learnt to live with the problem until, in his forties, his heart and lung showed signs of failure:

> In November 1984, I went to St Vincent's Hospital, Sydney, for assessment for a heart/lung transplant and, while there, was visited by the youth minister at a local church. My wife was attending this church and Alison, our eldest daughter, had begun attending also at the invitation of a friend of hers. I first attended the Christmas Day Service with my family and, because I was made to feel most welcome, I also began worshipping there.
>
> A visit by a group from Texas in 1985 was the time that I began seriously to question my relationship with God. At a men's dinner, someone spoke of his belief in Christ, his faith in the eternal life to follow and that, even if by some chance he was wrong, living a Christian life now would ensure a good life in this world. This to me seemed sound, logical reasoning.
>
> One night I went to church determined to follow Jesus. The feeling of joy and relief which came when I finally decided to do so is hard to adequately explain. As I was almost housebound awaiting a donor for transplant, I was more than able to study the material made available to me to build my faith.
>
> The peace and assurance that has followed since then has been a major factor in helping me and my family come through the traumas that have confronted us, including the transplant on 26 June 1987.

(e) *The tomb was empty.* The only likely explanation is that Jesus arose. Here are some alternative hypotheses to explain the empty tomb:

* *Jesus swooned but did not die.* This imaginative hypothesis is as old as Venturini and as new as the claims of Baigent, Leigh and Lincoln in their recent book, *The Holy Blood and the Holy Grail*.[46] This theory is at the heart of a 1990 Australian television documentary, 'The Riddle of the Dead Sea Scrolls', that focuses on the so-called 'poison theory' of Australian and International scholar, Dr Barbara Thiering.

  The assertion is that whilst Jesus was crucified, he did not die on the cross. He was placed in the tomb and the cool restfulness of this environment or other factors revived him. Despite the massive injuries he suffered — hit about the face with a staff, cruelly flogged, crucified with nails and a spear to the side — he boldly appeared in a few days pretending that he was resurrected. Even David Strauss, one of the great sceptics of yesteryear, has admitted that this theory is fanciful:

  It is impossible that a being who had stolen half dead out of the sepulchre, who crept about weak and ill wanting medical treatment, who required bandaging, strengthening and indulgence, and who still at last yielded to his sufferings could have given the disciples the impression that he was a conqueror over death and the grave, the Prince of life: an impression which lay at the bottom of their future ministry.[47]

* *The disciples stole the body.* Such fraudulent be-

haviour cannot be reconciled with the disciples' good character. Further, it is unreasonable to suggest that they would suffer persecution, martyrdom, ridicule and hardship for such a callous deception. Peter would hardly allow himself to be crucified upside down and John accept exile in Patmos for what they both knew was a lie.

* *Jewish or Roman authorities took the body.* It was not in the interest of either group to help inflame a legend about Jesus. They were about destroying Christianity, not enhancing its mystique.

* *The women went to the wrong tomb.* This could not be so. As we have already discussed, the women actually saw where Jesus was buried. There is not a whisper in antiquity of another tomb and, if Jesus was laid elsewhere, the authorities would have gleefully said so.

The empty tomb is good evidence. This is even more so when one realises that the resurrection of Jesus is far and away the most probable explanation for its non-occupancy. All this is circumstantial evidence in support of the case and a jury could not escape its significance. Sir Norman states: 'The empty tomb, then, forms a veritable rock on which all rationalistic theories of the resurrection dash themselves in vain.'[48]

❑ **Finding**
A few days after his death, Jesus of Nazareth was alive.

*   *   *

There is admissible, direct, documentary and circumstantial evidence that Jesus was dead at point A and alive at point B. The only logical inference is that Jesus was resurrected. The evidence overall is circumstantial, as no-one was actually there the moment Jesus arose. But, nevertheless, it is *substantial* evidence and would be sufficient to satisfy any court of law even if such a court held it required more evidence than normal, as the issue in dispute is not found in ordinary cases.

A question in reply

One can imagine a number of technical questions in response. It could be argued, for example, that yes, the case is very strong for Jesus' resurrection, but should we not dismiss it because a resurrection is a miracle?

This is the kind of approach the famous eighteenth century philosopher David Hume took. He developed his natural law argument against miracles on the basis of their uniqueness, maintaining one should always seek a *natural* explanation and avoid a conclusion that rests on the supernatural. So should we not settle for some other verdict?

I believe the answer is *No!* We cannot retreat from the overwhelming evidence for Jesus' resurrection *simply because* of an anti-supernatural bias. The law would not allow this. The case must be decided on the facts, no matter what they declare.

Thomas Sherlock lived in the same era as Hume and was Bishop of London and Master of the Temple Church, a church for lawyers. He showed much legal insight and common sense when he wrote:

A man rising from the grave is an object of sense
and can give the same evidence of his being alive as
any other man in the world can give. So that a
resurrection considered only as a fact to be proved
by evidence is a plain case; it requires no greater
ability in the witnesses than that they be able to
distinguish between a man dead and a man alive: a
point in which I believe every man living thinks
himself a judge.[49]

Another question that sometimes surfaces is that,
even if we acknowledge the resurrection occurred,
should we not leave it in 'supra-history'? That
means, should we not place it in a category where it
cannot be historically investigated and leave it
simply as a matter of faith? After all, unlike other
historical events, there is no human causation.

One cannot hide the resurrection in a faith box or
in a presuppositional way dismiss it because there is
no natural cause. The Gospel writers claim the
resurrection happened in time and space, in history.
Jesus ate, was touched and physically appeared.

For a lawyer like Sir Norman, the resurrection is
open to investigation like any other alleged historical fact. It either happened out there or it did not,
and the facts declare unequivocally that Jesus lived,
died and rose again in our material world. No 'soft'
option is possible.

Conclusion – a mammal that lays eggs

As the eighteenth century drew to a close, the
Western world encountered the platypus. It was a
furry, rabbit-sized, webbed, duck-billed animal that
had reproduction functions like a reptile and
roamed the rivers of the newly colonised eastern

Australia. When a platypus skin reached Europe, it was greeted with amazement. Its fur pointed to it being a mammal, but what about the flat beak and webbed feet? The platypus seemed so bizarre that many in London dismissed the skin as a farce and said the platypus was a hoax.

Then the zoologists in Europe heard that it was also alleged that this monster laid *eggs*. No mammal lays eggs! Most dismissed all reports of egg laying until, in 1884, a female was shot just after she had laid an egg and a second was found inside her body. The zoologists were astounded.

Great minds refused to accept the platypus' existence and others doubted the claims about what it could do. The problem was it did not fit some people's view of how the world operated, so they rejected it and they reached their verdict *even though the weight of evidence said otherwise.* Now the platypus, the animal many said could not be, can be viewed in any Australian zoo.

The platypus reminds one of the resurrection. Many refuse to accept it because it doesn't fit their world view, even though the evidence is overwhelming. Jesus was dead at point A and alive at point B. After careful examination we have to go with the facts even if they support something unusual. The platypus lives. . . and Jesus arose.

Endnotes:

1. Norman Anderson, *An Adopted Son: The Story of My Life*, IVP, 1985, p.18

2. *Ibid*. This book contains much honest biographical material.

3. *Contemporary Authors*, New Revision Series, 4, p.25

4. J.N.D. Anderson, *The Evidence for the Resurrection*, IVF, 1966, pp. 27-28

5. Sir Norman Anderson, *Jesus Christ: The Witness of History*, IVP, 1985; Sir Norman Anderson *Christianity and World Religions: The Challenge of Pluralism*, IVP, 1984; Sir Norman Anderson, *A Lawyer among the Theologians*, Hodder and Stoughton, 1973; Sir Norman Anderson, *The Teaching of Jesus*, IVP, 1983 and Sir Norman Anderson, *The Evidence for the Resurrection*, IVF, 1966

6. Sir Norman Anderson, *Christianity and World Religions: The Challenge of Pluralism*, p.47

7. Matthew 26, verse 47 to chapter 27, verse 31; Mark 14, verse 43 to chapter 15, verse 21; Luke 22, verse 47 to chapter 23, verse 25 and John 18, verse 1 to chapter 19, verse 16

8. David K. Breed, *The Trial of Christ from a Legal and Scriptural Viewpoint*, Baker, 1982, pp. 40-43

9. Sir Leslie Herron, *The Trial of Jesus of Nazareth from a Lawyer's Point of View*, The Australian Lawyers Christian Fellowship, 1970, pp.4-6

10. Matthew 26, verses 62 to 66

11. Simon Greenleaf, *The Testimony of the Evangelists*, Baker, 1984, p.562

12. John 19, verses 28 to 35

13. Matthew 26, verses 56 to 75

14. Mark 15, verses 16 to 41

15. Matthew 27, verse 32 to chapter 28, verse 20

16. Luke 23, verse 49

17. Matthew 27, verses 55 to 61

18. John 3 and chapter 19, verses 38 to 42

19. Matthew 27, verses 26 to 50; John 20, verses 16 to 37

20. Isaiah 53, verse 5; Zechariah 12, verse 10

21. John 20, verses 1 to 8 and 19 to 23

22. John 20, verses 24 to 29

23. John 21, verse 24

24. Matthew 28, verses 18 to 20

25. Mark 16, verses 14 to 20

26. John 20, verse 19 to chapter 21, verse 23 and Matthew 28, verses 16 to 20

27. 1 Peter 1, verse 3 and chapter 3, verses 21 and 22; 2 Peter 1, verse 16

28. Luke 24, verses 36 to 48

29. John 11, verses 2 to 12

30. John 20, verses 10 to 18

31. Matthew 28, verses 1 to 10

32. Matthew 27, verses 55 to 61 and Matthew 28, verses 1 to 10

33. See Jewish expert Pinchas Lapide, *The Resurrection of Jesus*, Augsbury, 1983, pp.97-99

34. 1 Corinthians 15, verse 6

35. Sir Norman Anderson, *The Fact of Christ: Some of the Evidence*, IVP, 1979, p.5

36. 1 Corinthians 15, verse 7

37. Acts 9, verses 3 to 6; chapter 22, verses 6 to 10; and chapter 26, verses 12 to 18

38. 1 Corinthians 15, verse 8

39. Lord George Lyttleton, 'A Letter to Gilbert West', in *Observations of St Paul: Being an Argumentative and Rational Defense of the Christian Revelation*, Manning and Loring, 1800, p.3

40. John 7, verse 5

41. 1 Corinthians 15, verse 9

42. Edward P. Arnolds et al., *Eyewitness Testimony: Strategies and Tactics*, McGraw-Hill, 1984, p.400. See also Gerard Nash and C.K. Jaisimaha Rao, *Homicide: The Law and the Proofs*, Law Book Company, 1986, pp.158-162

43. For a good discussion see William Webster, *The Fitness of the Witnesses of the Resurrection of Christ Considered*, James Lacy, 1731, pp.2-20

44. J.N.D. Anderson, *The Evidence of the Resurrection*, pp.20-23

45. 1 Corinthians chapter 15

46. Michael Baigent et al., *The Holy Blood and the Holy Grail*, Jonathan Cape, 1982

47. David Friedrich Strauss, *The Life of Jesus for the People*, I, 2nd ed., William and Norgate, 1879, p.412

48. J.N.D.Anderson, *The Evidence for the Resurrection*, p.20
49. Thomas Sherlock, *The Tryal of the Witnesses of the Resurrection of Jesus*, J. Roberts, 1729, p.62. This book is photolithographically reproduced in John Warwick Montgomery (ed.), *Jurisprudence: A Book of Readings*, International Scholarly Publishers, 1974

7

Sir Lionel Luckhoo:
The world's 'most successful' lawyer

It may be true, but does it work?

RECORDS ARE MADE to be broken! But there is one record that appears unbeatable. It is defence lawyer Sir Lionel Luckhoo's remarkable achievement of 245 successive murder acquittals. Admittedly, a handful of Sir Lionel's clients were found guilty by a jury, but these decisions were overturned by judges on appeal.

The Guinness Book of Records lists this advocate from Guyana as the world's 'most successful' lawyer.[1] Understandably, most lawyers are speechless when they first hear of Sir Lionel's legal feats — here is an actual, 'true to life' Perry Mason!

The reasons for Sir Lionel's triumphs are numerous. He was born in 1914 into a legal environment, his father being the first Indian solicitor in Guyana. Law seems to have been in the blood, two of Sir Lionel's brothers being Queen's Counsels and lawyers of standing.

Sir Lionel is a fastidious practitioner who personally interviews his clients and their witnesses and he always visits the scene of the crime. Clearly he is capable of handling the immense pressure of knowing a defendant's life is resting on his advocacy. Further, he has never lost the common touch and has the ability to recall in detail the evidence given during a case.

One courtroom technique that has aided Sir Lionel was passed on to him by his father the night before his first murder trial:

> Pick out two individuals. Look for one who is nodding his head and seems to be agreeing with you; then seek out another who is turning his head away because you do not convince him. Speak first to the one who is nodding. When you think you have won him over completely, move on to the one who appears dubious. Concentrate on him, look him in the eye, make him feel that you are eschewing everything else to hold his attention because the life of your client is in his hands and that he must be convinced, as he ought to be convinced, that your man is innocent and deserves an acquittal.[2]

The lifetime achievements of this amazing man extend beyond his fame before a jury. He was appointed a Queen's Counsel in 1954, was the head of four trade unions, was a member of Guyana's Legislative Council before independence and was elected mayor of Georgetown, Guyana, on four occasions.

He was a diplomat of international note. He was involved in the negotiations for the independence of both Guyana and Barbados. Then an extraordinary event occurred. Sir Lionel was appointed as High Commissioner for Guyana and Barbados in Britain as well as being appointed as ambassador for both countries. Another record: it was the first time a person had been appointed to serve two sovereign territories at such high levels. It created a diplomatic storm and Queen Elizabeth would often ask, 'Which hat are you wearing today, Sir Lionel?'[3]

He practised as a barrister in England, served as a judge of the Supreme Court in Guyana, was knighted twice by the Queen and was president of the Guyana Olympic Association from 1974 to 1979.

Sir Lionel knew disappointment, too. His early tertiary studies in London were in medicine, but he could not stand the sight of blood. He has faced the sadness of a broken marriage. He has known defeat at the polls when seeking political office.

One tragic moment for him was his acting in a custody case for the infamous Jim Jones of Jonestown. On one occasion, Jones threatened to kill the boy who was the subject of the dispute, as well as himself. Sir Lionel, speaking on a radio in Georgetown some 150 miles away, talked Jones out of it. A little later this cult messiah shocked the world when he arranged the shooting of a US congressman and 'persuaded' 900 of his own followers to drink cyanide.

The former Prime Minister of Guyana, L.F.S. Burnham, is a friend of Sir Lionel as well as a political colleague and opponent. He has said that Sir Lionel 'is undoubtedly one of Guyana's most outstanding sons'.[4] When one looks at Sir Lionel's achievements, it would be fair to say that that praise is most warranted and indeed he has proved to be among the most capable and interesting lawyers/diplomats of modern times.

Yet Sir Lionel, who had a nominal Christian commitment, realised in 1978 that all his accomplishments had still not satisfied:

> I had no peace. Peace comes from God and belongs to him. I never went to the Prince of peace, to Jesus to seek peace, until one day... I invited Jesus to come into my life as my Lord and Saviour. It was the first time I have ever so invited him. That was it! It was in a hotel! The transformation was immediate. From that day my life changed — I moved from death to life, from darkness to light. I was born again. My life took a 180° change. I found real peace and happiness and joy and righteousness and holiness.[5]

The world's 'most successful' lawyer gave his life unreservedly to Jesus Christ, leaving all to go around the world to speak about him. The resurrection of Jesus was central to this commitment:

> I have spent more than forty-two years as a defence trial lawyer appearing in many parts of the world and am still in active practice. I have been fortunate to secure a number of successes in jury trials and I say unequivocally the evidence for the resurrection of Jesus Christ is so overwhelming that it compels acceptance by proof which leaves absolutely no room for doubt.[6]

Of the eyewitnesses to that event, he says:

> Do you think [they] were lying? If so, for what reward? For torture and for death? He spoke to

them; he ate with them. Clearly, they were telling
the truth about an unmistakable fact that
manifested to them as to make the whole Roman
Empire unable to shake their testimony or stem the
tide of their evangelism.[7]

One of the simplest and best pamphlets on
Christianity is Sir Lionel's *What is Your Verdict?* He
has written a number of other tracts along similar
lines. His biography, *Sir Lionel*, discusses many of
his cases and gives much insight into this man.[8]

Does commitment to Jesus Christ work?

People want to know not only if something is true,
but whether it *works*. We have considered the testimony that confirms the life, death and resurrection
of Jesus and, by so doing, have stimulated our
minds.

However, we are whole people and there is more
to life than legal evidence and the cognitive. If Jesus
is the truth, we would expect him to touch our basic
human needs and enable us to experience some of
the joy and liberation he claims to bring. Sir Lionel
discovered the peace he was searching for. What
are some of the other privileges that belong to those
who acknowledge Jesus Christ as Lord?

(a) *Strength*. Life was not meant to be easy! Often
we wonder why we bother. Jesus offers strength for
the living of life. The apostle Paul declared, 'I can
do anything through [Jesus] who gives me
strength.'[9] This was not an empty cry. In 2 Corinthians 11, verse 16 to chapter 12, verse 10, we read
how Paul faced severe emotional, physical and
spiritual struggles and yet he could still proclaim:

'That is why, for Christ's sake, I delight in weakness, in insults, in hardships, in persecution, in difficulties. For when I am weak, then I am strong.' Christ brings strength for the tough days.

(b) *Defeat of anxiety.* This is an era of stress. Our world changes quickly and much is uncertain. Is there a resting place for an anxious spirit? The apostle Peter who knew both fear and failure exhorted, 'Cast all your anxiety on him because he cares for you.'[10]

(c) *Friendship.* Loneliness darts into our lives in times of grief, separation from loved ones and when there is friction in relationships. It is a common experience. The writer of Hebrews reminds us that God gives us this promise: 'Never will I leave you; never will I forsake you.' The resurrected Jesus, the One who came to reveal God the Father, offers us his constant companionship.[11]

(d) *Inner satisfaction.* In the last few years Western society has experienced a massive disillusionment with materialism as the answer to life. It simply has not satisfied, particularly as the Western world is thrust into deeper recession. People are searching for a spiritual dimension to life. Peter, in the first Christian sermon ever preached, promised the presence of God within all those who follow Jesus: 'And you will receive the gift of the Holy Spirit.'[12]

Paul reminds us what tangible benefits the Holy Spirit brings to our lives: 'The fruit of the Spirit is love, joy, peace, patience, kindness, goodness, faithfulness, gentleness and self control'.[13] Jesus, not New Age philosophy, Eastern mysticism or the pursuit of materialism, is alone capable of quenching our inner longing, sense of cosmic orphanhood and search for meaning.[14]

(e) *Beyond the why.* How often do we experience things that we cannot understand— a tragedy, a failure, persecution or a broken relationship? A disciple of Jesus does not have all the answers, nor are they excluded from hurts, but they can live beyond the 'why', because they can discern a deeper purpose to life's inexplicable events and mysteries.

As the apostle Paul reminds us: '. . .in all things God works for the good of those who love him.'[15] A Christian realises God takes our disappointments and produces good even out of evil. That is a tremendous promise.

(f) *Forgiveness.* Guilt and sin are enormous problems. We know we have fallen and that we are in need of mercy. In Jesus, there is acceptance and complete forgiveness.

In that first Christian sermon, we are told to repent — admit our failures and turn from them — in order that 'your sins may be forgiven'.[16] Guilt and failure are dealt with when we hand ourselves to Jesus as he paid the price for us on the cross. Unlike other religions, Christianity rests on an act of love and we do not face the frustration of trying to earn our salvation through good deeds. No matter what we have done, Jesus is there for us.

(g) *Certainty.* Many people give themselves to a religion and remain children of doubt. The Bible promises that if we truly hand ourselves to God, he will bring us conviction that Jesus is the answer.[17]

(h) *Servanthood.* The wider society is consumed by 'me-ism'. Such an ideology is without compassion and a heart for justice. It is not real in the face of so much oppression and poverty.

To be a servant to others is a rich experience and is the only authentic way to live. Jesus is the perfect model and motivation for servanthood. Jesus said, 'My command is this: Love each other as I have loved you. Greater love has no-one than this, that he lay down his life for his friends.'[18]

(i) *Eternal life.* Death is a universal enemy. It is humanity's ultimate tragedy. However, it need not be the end; rather it can be the opening to a new beginning — a point made in this verse: 'For God so loved the world that he gave his one and only Son, that whoever believes in him shall not perish but have eternal life.'[19]

Eternal life speaks of a quality of existence that is never ending — a life minus pain, tears, disorder and mourning.[20] It is a life we can be certain of as Jesus, by his resurrection, showed that there is life beyond the grave.[21]

(j) *Guidance.* Today people are looking for guidance, for absolutes on which they can base their life. A Christian has direction in the Bible and it can be trusted. Let me explain:

* The Gospels, as we have seen, are reliable historical documents.

* In the Gospels, Jesus claims to be one with God the Father — in fact, God himself.[22]

* The Gospels record the perfect life, miracles and resurrection of Jesus, proving that he is indeed divine.[23]

* Jesus stated that the Old Testament was totally trustworthy[24] and he implied this for the New

Testament, as he indicated that more than human hands would produce it.[25] The apostle Paul sums this up in this way:

> All scripture is God-breathed and is useful for teaching, rebuking, correcting and training in righteousness, so that the man of God may be thoroughly equipped for every good work.[26]

Sir Lionel's words at an Australian press conference well summarise the points made about life with Jesus:

> Why have I come to Australia? Well, if Dr Salk had kept quiet about the vaccine he had discovered to help polio sufferers, what a tragedy that would have been! And when I have found Jesus to be the answer to the problems we have, both personal and national, I must share it with others.[27]

A question in reply

'We live in a global village and many religions/ideologies, like eastern mysticism and New Age, apparently offer satisfaction. Why should we follow Christ and limit ourselves to him?'

This is a common objection to the exclusivity of Christianity. The reason we should trust Jesus as the way, the truth and the life is that he gives verification of his claims. The resurrection of Jesus is the foundation of the Christian faith. If the resurrection indeed happened, then Jesus is what he claimed to be. Is it wise to listen to those who still occupy the grave and offer no tangible proof for the truth of what they taught and stood for?

You may be a student of philosophy. If so, you

may be asking what about Lessing's axiom: 'the accidental truths of history can never become the proof of necessary truths of reason'?[28] In other words, rationalists assert that as history, unlike mathematics, is not 100 per cent certain, historical events, like the resurrection, should never be the basis for a system of thought, a religion.

In answer to this, it must be asserted that a meaningful faith will involve a tangible, evidential verification, otherwise who knows if our religion, our inner experience and our belief system is true? And such a verification can only be probable.

With so many world views, I vote for the one with a God-given verification: the resurrection of Jesus.

Endnotes:

1. *The Guinness Book of Records*, 1990, p.211
2. Fred Archer, *Sir Lionel*, Gift Publications, 1980, p.33
3. *Ibid*, p.161
4. *Ibid*, Foreword
5. Sir Lionel Luckhoo, *What is Your Verdict?*, Fellowship Press, 1984, p.19
6. Lionel Luckhoo, *The Question Answered: Did Jesus Rise from the Dead?*, n.p., n.d.
7. Sir Lionel Luckhoo, *What is your Verdict?*, p.12
8. Fred Archer, *op.cit.*, and Sir Lionel Luckhoo, *What is Your Verdict?*
9. Philippians 4, verse 13
10. 1 Peter 2, verse 7
11. Hebrews 13, verse 5
12. Acts 2, verse 38
13. Galatians 5, verses 22 and 23
14. John chapter 4
15. Romans 8, verse 28
16. Acts 2, verse 38
17. John 7, verses 16 and 17
18. John 15, verses 12 and 13
19. John 3, verse 16
20. Revelation 22, verse 4
21. 1 Corinthians chapter 15
22. Matthew 11, verse 27; John 10, verse 30 and chapter 12, verse 45; Matthew 26, verses 62 to 66; Matthew 9, verses 1 to 8
23. John 20, verses 28 and 31 and Romans 1, verse 4
24. Matthew 5, verses 17 to 19
25. John 14, verses 26 and 27; John 16, verses 12 to 15; Acts 1, verses 21 to 26
26. 2 Timothy 3, verses 16 and 17
27. *New Life*, 8 October 1981
28. See *The Encyclopedia of Philosophy*, 4, pp.444-445

8

Dr Frank Morison:
A case of mistaken identity

What should our response be to Jesus?

ONE OF THE MOST POPULAR Christian books of this
century is Frank Morison's *Who Moved the Stone?*[1]
The work is a readable sketch of the events up until
the burial of Jesus. Frank Morison then comes to
the conclusion that the tomb was empty, because
Christ arose.

Frank Morison, contrary to popular opinion, was
not a lawyer and in fact that name is a pseudonym,
his legal name being Albert Henry Ross.[2] Ross
lived from 1881 to 1950 and made his home in London. In his youth, he attended Shakespeare's old
grammar school at Stratford-on-Avon and he later
became a prolific writer. He worked for many years
at the S.H. Benson advertising agency, becoming
managing director. His other work of note is a short
fantasy called *Sunset*.[3]

What does a non-lawyer add to our legal case?
Frank Morison is included here for two essential
reasons:

(a) *His book illustrates how simple it is to apply legal investigative skills.* Anyone can effectively use the pages of this book. Morison used investigative skills so well that readers and scholars alike wrongly assumed he was a lawyer. His work has enabled other lawyers to do the same.

(b) *His book demonstrates that the message of Jesus as recorded in the Gospels can challenge even the most sceptical mind.* Frank Morison did not commence his research as a Christian. As someone wedded to German 'negative higher biblical criticism' and scientific rationalism, he set out to write a monograph which would discredit the 'primitive' stories surrounding Jesus' last days. Certainly, he had a high regard for Jesus as a person, but he felt the miraculous side of his life was 'suspect'.

As Frank Morison carried out his research into the historical character of the Gospels, a strange thing occurred. He started to become convicted about the truth of the Jesus story and he finished up writing a Christian classic. These two quotes reveal his final verdict on the resurrection:

No great moral structure like the early church, characterised as it was by lifelong persecution and personal suffering, could have reared its head on a statement that every one of the eleven apostles knew to be a lie. . .

There may be and, as the writer thinks, there certainly is a deep and profoundly historical basis for that much disputed sentence in the Apostles' Creed — 'The *third day* he rose again from the dead.'[4]

Throughout these pages we have demonstrated

that Jesus lived, died and rose again — it happened. We have established the resurrection proves that Jesus is both God and Saviour. We have openly dealt with the problems and the questions people raise. Lawyers have been called and explained the evidence for us.

Now the ultimate question is: What do you think of Jesus? You are the judge and jury! It is time for your honest finding even if you, like Frank Morison and me, have to change your mind. This book has been a plea to follow the evidence wherever it leads and whatever it costs.

And remember, as Socrates has said, 'the unexamined life is not worth living'.[5]

*   *   *

Endnotes:

1.   Frank Morison, *Who Moved the Stone?*, IVP, 1982
2.   For full details see Ross Richard Clifford, *The Case of Eight Legal Apologists for the Defense of Scripture and the Christ Event*, thesis, Simon Greenleaf School of Law, Anaheim, 1987, pp. 129-134
3.   Frank Morison, *Sunset*, Century, 1932
4.   Frank Morison, *Who Moved the Stone?*, pp.89 and 193
5.   Socrates, cited in Plato's *Apology*

Appendix 1:

Lawyers' statements on the resurrection

HERE IS A SELECTION OF STATEMENTS lawyers, other than those already discussed, have made about the Gospels and the resurrection:

(a) *David K. Breed* was a St Louis, USA lawyer and author of the excellent book, *The Trial of Christ: From a Legal and Scriptural Viewpoint*:

> The death of Christ as the sacrifice of God for man is the greatest fact in the story of salvation, except his glorious resurrection. . . sentence was passed by a prejudiced court without a diligent inquiry into the merits of the case. . . if the Sanhedrin had really heard and honestly weighed the evidence they would have concluded that Christ is the Messiah — is our Redeemer![1]

(b) *Walter Marion Chandler* was a New York attorney in the early decades of the twentieth century who had an outstanding reputation. His two- volume book, *The Trial of Jesus from a Lawyer's Point of View*, 1908, is one of the best and most comprehensive on this subject.

In this work he wrote:

> When we come to summarise, we are led to declare that, if the Gospel historians be not worthy of belief, we are

without foundation for rational faith in the secular annals of the human race. No other literature bears historic scrutiny so well as the New Testament biographies. . . I believe that Jesus was divine and that if he was not divine, Divinity has not touched this globe. I base my conviction of this fact upon the perfect purity, beauty and sinlessness of Jesus; upon the overwhelming historical evidence of his resurrection from the dead. . . as well as upon the evident impress of a divine hand upon genuine Christian civilisation in every age.[2]

(c) *Sir Edward Clarke*, a former King's Counsel, wrote the following:

As a lawyer I have made a prolonged study of the evidences for the events of the first Easter Day. To me the evidence is conclusive, and over and over again in the High Court I have secured the verdict on evidence not nearly so compelling. Inference follows on evidence, and a truthful witness is always artless and disdains effect. The Gospel evidence for the resurrection is of this class and, as a lawyer, I accept it unreservedly as the testimony of truthful men to facts they were able to substantiate.[3]

(d) *Charles Colson* is a lawyer and was Special Counsel to President Richard Nixon. He became involved in the political scandal, Watergate, gave his life to Christ and is the founder of Prison Fellowship. He wrote:

Take it from one who was inside the Watergate web looking out, who saw firsthand how vulnerable a cover-up is: Nothing less than a witness as awesome as the resurrected Christ could have caused those men to maintain to their dying whispers that Jesus is alive and Lord.[4]

(e) *Dale Foreman*, a graduate of Harvard Law School and a lawyer in Washington State, is author of *Crucify Him: A Lawyer Looks at the Trial of Jesus*:

These facts [the trial, crucifixion and death of Christ], I believe, are clear and proven beyond a reasonable doubt. Whether you can take one step further and believe the miracle of his resurrection is something only you can decide. Still, the reliability of the rest of the Gospel is so plain that it is but a small step to believe in the resurrected Christ. And what's more, it would be hard to believe that a man could have such an influence on the world if he had not overcome the ultimate enemy — death.

The teachings of Jesus have changed the world. In 2000 years not a day has gone by when the influence of this itinerant teacher from Nazareth has not been felt. As a trial lawyer, trained to be rational, skeptical and critical, I believe it improbable that any fraud or false Messiah could have made such a profound impression for good. The most reasonable conclusion, and the most satisfying, is that Jesus was indeed the Son of God, that he was who he claimed to be and that he did come back to life.[5]

(f)   *Val Grieve* is a senior partner in a Manchester, England, firm of solicitors. He is the author of the book, *Your Verdict on the Empty Tomb of Jesus*:

Ever since I became a Christian, I have carefully examined the evidence for the resurrection, the physical return from the dead of Jesus Christ. My purpose in writing this book is to present this evidence to you. I claim that logic must point in the direction of his resurrection on an actual day and date in our history when, if you had been there, you could have touched the living Jesus and heard him speak.[6]

(g)   *Hugo Grotius* (1583–1645) was a Dutch lawyer, scholar, Swedish Ambassador to the French Court, theologian and the father of International Law.

When discussing why certain people of learning had become followers of Christ, he remarked:

There can be no reason given but this one; that upon diligent inquiry such as becomes prudent men to take. . . they found, that the report which was spread abroad, concerning the miracles that were done by him, was true and founded upon sufficient testimony.[7]

(h) *Sir Matthew Hale* was Lord Chief Justice in the reign of Charles II. He wrote:

[God the Father] sent his Son into the world, to take upon him human nature and to become man for our sakes. . . and to give us all the assurance possible for the truth of that message, by his holy life, by his miracles, by his death, resurrection and ascension into heaven.[8]

(i) *Sir Leslie Herron* was Chief Justice of NSW, Australia. In an address given on Palm Sunday, 1970, he stated:

Let any objective reader put side by side the four Gospels and add to them the account in Acts of the Apostles and he will be struck, as any judge accustomed to evaluate evidence is always struck, with one outstanding fact. It is this: that while there may be a great variety of detail or form of expression or narration of or emphasis put on occurrences, underneath it all, the substance and weight of the narration are true.[9]

(j) *Francis Lamb* was a lawyer from Wisconsin, USA, who wrote the work, *Miracle and Science*, which examines Bible miracles by legal tests:

Tested by the standards and ordeals of jural science by which questions of fact are ascertained and demonstrated in contested questions of right between man and man in courts of justice, *the resurrection of Jesus stands a demonstrated fact.*[10]

(k) *Irwin H. Linton* was a Washington lawyer who wrote a number of best selling Christian books in the first half of this century:

The *prima facie improbability* of divine paternity or
supernatural origin of men of whom no other
supernatural feature is proved or even asserted is as
strong as in the *prima facie probability* of such an origin
for a man whose supernatural words are
self-evidencing miracles before us and whose
superhuman deeds and resurrection from the dead are
proved as are no other facts in the history of the world.[11]

(l) *Lord Lyndhurst* was Solicitor General, Attorney
General and three times High Chancellor of England.
Upon his death, among his personal papers were found
this comment:

I know pretty well what evidence is; and I tell you, such
evidence as that for the resurrection has never broken
down yet.[12]

(m) *Frank J. Powell* was an English magistrate and barrister and author of the outstanding scholarly work, *The
Trial of Jesus Christ*, in which he wrote:

Today, as always, the Cross of Christ both condemns
and saves mankind. Jesus was the symbolic as well as
the representative man. He personified goodness,
righteousness and truth. Arrayed against him were the
forces of evil – religious bigotry, love of material power,
narrow nationalism, the cynicism of the intellectuals
and human selfishness. Might appeared to triumph
over right. Few, if any, of those who took part in the
tragic events of the 14–15th day of Nisan (April, c.AD 30)
realised that Jesus embodied the force that could
transform the world. None had any consciousness that
Jesus was ushering in a new era, a new way of life and
attitude to God founded on a realisation of the
Fatherhood of God and the brotherhood of regenerate
man — with himself as 'the Way'.[13]

(n) *Stephen D. Williams* was a Detroit, USA lawyer and
author of the popular book, *The Bible in Court or Truth*

vs. Error, in which he wrote:

> We have been asked many times if the proof of the
> resurrection of Jesus was as complete and convincing
> from a legal standpoint, as that afforded by the record of
> the other events in his life narrated in the Gospel. To
> this question we must answer: Yes. The proof is to be
> found in the same record, supplied by the same
> witnesses. . .[14]

(o) *Sir Hendrik Rutgers* is a Sydney solicitor, a former Deputy Judge Advocate of the Court Martial,
Indonesia and he has been honoured by the
Queens of the Netherlands and Great Britain. He
wrote:

> I know when I am spiritually thirsty, God will quench
> my thirst. . . I want to testify that I believe in Jesus
> Christ. . . our only Saviour. . .I believe in the Holy Spirit
> who was given to us after the resurrection of Jesus.[15]

(p) *Herbert C. Casteel* retired as a lawyer and judge
in 1989. He has served as Mayor of the City of
Carthage, Missouri, USA. He wrote of the resurrection and the claims of Christianity:

> We do not have to take an irrational leap of faith. God
> has given us the evidence. Christianity is the truth.[16]

(q) *James C. McRuer*, former Chief Justice of the
High Court of Ontario, Canada declared:

> At the ninth hour Jesus was dead. It remained for the
> commander of the Roman guard to give the final verdict
> on the day's miscarriage of justice: certainly this man
> was innocent![17]

Endnotes:

1. David K. Breed, *The Trial of Christ from a Legal and Scriptural Standpoint*, Baker, 1982, pp.9 and 60-61
2. Walter M. Chandler, *The Trial of Christ from a Lawyer's Standpoint*, I, Federal Book Co., 1925, pp.67 and 211
3. Cited in John R.W. Stott, *Basic Christianity*, IVP, 1974, p.47
4. Charles Colson, *Loving God*, Marshalls, 1984, p.69
5. Dale Foreman, *Crucify Him: A Lawyer looks at the trial of Jesus*, Zondervan, 1990, pp.176 and 178
6. Val Grieve, *Your Verdict*, STL/IVP, 1988, p.17
7. Hugo Grotius, *The Truth of the Christian Religion*, rev. ed., William Baynes & Son, 1825, p.82
8. Sir Matthew Hale, *A Letter of Advice to his Grand-children*, 2nd ed., Taylor and Hessey, 1823, p.45
9. Sir Leslie Herron, *The Trial of Jesus of Nazareth from a Lawyer's Point of View*, The Australian Lawyer's Christian Fellowship, 1970, p.1
10. Francis J. Lamb, *Miracle and Science: Bible Miracles Examined by the Methods, Rules and Tests of the Science of Jurispudence as Administered Today in Courts of Justice*, Bibliotheca Sacra, 1909, p.284
11. Irwin H. Linton, *The Sanhedrin Verdict*, Loizeaux Brothers, 1943, p.18
12. Cited in Josh McDowell, *The Resurrection Factor*, Here's Life, 1981, p.12
13. Frank J. Powell, *The Trial of Jesus Christ*, Paternoster, 1952, pp.152-153
14. Stephen D. Williams, *The Bible in Court or Truth vs Error*, Dearborn, 1925, p.212
15. Sir Hendrick Rutgers, *Testimony of a Lawyer*, Hexagon Press, 1992, p.142
16. Herbert C. Casteel, *Beyond a Reasonable Doubt*, College Press, 1990, p.200
17. James C. McRuer, *This Man was Innocent*, Clarke, Irwin, 1978, p.76

Appendix 2:

Mr Clarrie Briese's statement
on the resurrection

MR CLARRIE BRIESE is a distinguished Australian. He
was born in the NSW country town of Temora in 1930.
He studied law and qualified as a barrister in 1961.

In 1971, he graduated Bachelor of Arts from Sydney
University, majoring in government and English literature. In 1976 he was awarded a Churchill Fellowship to
the United Kingdom to study alternatives to imprisonment. He received the Diploma of Criminology from
Cambridge University in 1977. From 1979 to 1990, he
was the Chief Magistrate of NSW. He is now Commissioner, NSW Crime Commission.

As Chief Magistrate, Clarrie Briese was known for
his integrity and honesty. The present independence of
magistrates from executive government is in no small
way due to his endeavours.

The following is an extract from his popular
apologetic, *Witnesses to the Resurrection — Credible or
Not*:

> Two thousand years ago, a man called Jesus Christ was
> born into the world and lived in a country which we
> know today as Israel. This is an historical fact, accepted

by all. Why? Because the historical records of the past, most of them compiled by followers of Jesus Christ, but others also by non-Christians, testify to that. They clearly demonstrate the existence of the man Jesus Christ. The records show that this man Jesus commenced his public ministry at the age of thirty years.

That ministry continued for a relatively short period of three years, during which time he claimed to be sent from God. Indeed, he claimed to be the Messiah, that special messenger from God whom the Jewish nation, through the prophecies of the Old Testament scriptures, had been expecting for centuries. Throughout his short three year ministry, he spoke and did things as though he were God. Furthermore, he himself made the staggering claim, not only that he was God's promised Messiah, but that he was the eternal Son of the Triune Godhead. that is, God himself!

Now we would all agree that to claim to be God is a pretty staggering claim for a human being to make. People who make claims like that today are dismissed by us as mad or eccentric. We in the courts put many of them in mental institutions, diagnosing them to be suffering from schizophrenia or paranoia.

But this man Jesus cannot be so easily dismissed in that way. In a relatively short period of time after his death, his followers changed the world. And today they are still influencing and changing it. His immediate disciples became convinced that he was and is the God of this world, that the world was in fact created through him. They recognised him as the promised Messiah of the Old Testament and they finally realised that in him lay the truth, the absolute key to life.

They established a movement which we know as Christianity. This movement quickly spread through and enveloped the then known world. It came to dominate and shape the whole of Western civilisation, including its institutions. It penetrated and continues today to penetrate the whole of the world with its message of reconciliation of humankind to God through the redemptive death of Jesus, God's messenger to the world. Christianity has adherents — many unfortunately in name only — numbering hundreds of millions throughout the world.

Now the reason that Jesus' immediate followers were finally convinced that Jesus was what he claimed to be, namely God, was, as they tell us, that they were eyewitnesses to the monumentally staggering fact that Jesus, whom they saw to have been dead and buried, had risen from the dead. They saw and experienced this. It was for them a mind-shattering event. And no wonder. It clearly and finally demonstrated to them that his claim to have been not just a mere man but God in human flesh was in fact the truth. At least that is their evidence.

Now if this evidence of these witnesses is true, not only must it be the fact that there is a God of this world, but he must be found and can only be found in the person and ministry of Jesus Christ. It further follows that you and I are not accidents in the world, arriving here by chance. We are the creation of an Almighty God and therefore accountable to that God.

Well now, all of what I have just said depends on the reliability of the witnesses to Jesus and his resurrection.

[*Clarrie Briese then examines the witnesses, using tests similar to those of Simon Greenleaf and Walter Chandler.*]

At the end of our examination, putting the witnesses through Judge Chandler's five tests, one is left to say that the only rational conclusion is that the witnesses to the resurrection of Jesus Christ are witnesses of the highest credibility. If we are unable to accept their histories, why would we accept the histories of any other incident of the human race?. . .

Now if Jesus has been raised from the dead and is alive today, what does that mean for you and me? That is the big question, isn't it? It is the question which the immediate disciples of Jesus had to ask themselves, and to do some careful thinking about under the guidance of his Spirit.

We can read the result of that thinking in their magnificent letters to the various Christian churches, letters which now form part of the Christian Bible. Have you read them? Have you read the four Gospels?

If you haven't, you owe it to yourself to do so. You will discover that the disciples' understanding of the Old Testament scriptures had to be reorientated, had to take into account this incredible new fact of history, the resurrection of Jesus.

When first confronted with this fact, they were initially staggered, dumbfounded. Some of them couldn't believe it to be true — for example, Thomas. But when the truth did finally bear in on them and they knew it to be a fact through their own senses, their reaction was one of enormous joy. And no wonder! Jesus was their personal Lord, their Redeemer! They now recognised fully who he was, the scales fell from their eyes and they understood what the prophecies of the Old Testament scriptures had been saying.

And mind-boggling as it was, they knew that these prophecies had been fulfilled before their very eyes. Jesus was that Messiah whom God through the centuries of history of the Old Testament period had promised to send to his people in the fullness of time. They came to understand that Jesus had come to redeem not only the Jewish people, but the Gentiles as well — that is, the whole of humankind. And they had actually seen it happen; they were witnesses — eyewitnesses.[1]

Endnote:

1. This tract is not published, but a copy on receipt of postage is available from Legal Apologists, 2–4 Tea Gardens Avenue, Kirrawee, NSW 2232, Australia

Appendix 3:

The Gospels in court

WE HAVE SEEN HOW LAWYERS affirm that the Gospels of Matthew, Mark, Luke and John are trustworthy, historical documents. They reach their finding after applying general legal principles that obtain to documents and the testimony of witnesses. These show that the Gospels are a solid foundation on which to base one's faith. We could rest our case here.

Some prominent legal apologists, like Professor Simon Greenleaf, Walter Chandler and Dr Montgomery, go further and suggest that the Gospels could actually be admitted *today* in a court of law.[1] This is a somewhat academic question: whether it is true or not does not impact the reliability of the case made to-date. But if the Gospels could be admitted, that would be just one more nail in the coffin of scepticism.

Let's look at some brief arguments in support of the Gospels being so accepted.[2]

A hypothetical case
In the country of Oz it has become an offence by law to name any tertiary institution after a non-historical figure. Christ College is so prosecuted. In their defence, the ruling College Council plead that Jesus Christ was

historical.

When an historical statement such as 'Jesus of Nazareth in or about 4 BC to AD 35 lived in the region of Galilee' is in dispute, a judge in his discretion can rely on his own historical knowledge. The judge, where appropriate, can use historical reference works to aid him.

Without doubt in this case the historical references would include the non-Christian texts mentioned in the chapter on Lord Hailsham and the Gospels which we have shown to be historical texts. Under historical knowledge, the references the judge refers to are not admitted into evidence. But a judge today could consider the Gospels if he was asked to find on the historicity of Christ. In some jurisdictions, the court may take Judicial Notice of some fact after acquainting itself with the historical evidence.[3]

If the case went further and he Gospels definitely had to be admitted into evidence to support the argument for the historicity of Christ, the defence could refer to the American case, *Dallas County v Commercial Union Assurance Co.*

In this trial, the defendants produced a newspaper article more than fifty years old to support their position. It was a reporter's eyewitness account of a fire and this was the only substantial evidence on this issue in the case. The article was not rejected even though the reporter was not present to give evidence. The Federal Court of Appeal affirmed that the District Court was correct in admitting and relying on the newspaper report to prove the fire.

It was stated by the said Appeal Court:

> To our minds, the article published in the *Selma Morning Times* on the day of the fire is more reliable, more trustworthy, more competent evidence than the testimony of a witness called to the stand some fifty-eight years later... We do not characterise this

newspaper as a 'business record', nor as an 'ancient document', nor as any other readily identifiable and happily tagged species of hearsay exception. It is admissible because it is trustworthy, relevant and material, and its admission is within the trial judge's exercise of discretion in holding the hearing within reasonable bounds.[4]

The US court admitted the newspaper report and relied on its substance simply on basis of it being good reliable evidence. In its mind, that overcame any technical objections. The Gospels are likewise good, reliable evidence that address the facts in issue in our hypothetical case.

A question in reply

Some might be saying that, while there is historical knowledge and the American case, there is also the hearsay rule — that would ensure the Gospels would not be admitted in a court of law. Perhaps they would be used as an historical reference by a judge, but not admitted. Do you agree?

What is the common law hearsay rule? In the context of documents, it means that one cannot prove a fact by statements in a document without the witness being present to give evidence in support. In other words, oral evidence is needed as well, so that the writer of the document can be cross-examined as to what he saw and wrote. As Matthew, Mark, Luke and John could not be present in court to be quizzed on their writings, the Gospels are merely hearsay and not admissible.

Are the Gospels ruled out because of the hearsay rule? No. Why?

The hearsay rule operates in Anglo-American common law countries like USA, England and Australia. In many European countries and other countries that follow the Continental civil law tradition, there is much greater freedom over what is admitted and often the hearsay rule, or its equivalent, does not exist. They simply accept evidence that is good.

Even in Anglo-American law, there is precedent for admission of documentary evidence where no oral corroboration is available — as seen in the Dallas case. Many courts and commissions today are not willing to be bound by the technicalities of the 'hearsay rule', especially when the issue is determining truth rather than the trial of an individual. Further, legislators are passing statute law for the accepting of statements in documents where there is no oral support.

For example in England, there is the Civil Evidence Act 1968 and in the United States, the Federal Rules of Evidence Rule 803 (16) which declares an exception to the hearsay rule shall be 'Statements in ancient documents'.[5]

It is certain the hearsay rule will continue to be liberalised in its interpretation. The Honourable Adrian Roden QC, Assistant Commissioner, New South Wales (Australia) Commission against Corruption and retired Supreme Court Judge, had this to say to the Fourth International Anti-Corruption Conference:

> It is true that as a general rule hearsay is less reliable than direct evidence. But much that is strictly hearsay can be of value, while much that is direct and admissible evidence is not. . . The nonsense that the rule against hearsay can perpetrate was acknowledged by Lord Diplock in a rare piece of judicial candour about its artificiality, in *Jones v. Metcalfe* [1967] 1 W.L.R. @ 1290:
>
> > 'I have every sympathy for the justices because the inference of fact that the appellant was the driver. . . is irresistible as a matter of commonsense. But [the rule against hearsay] is a branch of the law that has little to do with commonsense.'

> The array of statutory exceptions now to be found in various jurisdictions is further evidence of the unsatisfactory nature of the rule.[6]

In Anglo-American common law countries, there is as well the 'Ancient Documents Rule'. There are exceptions to the rule that hearsay evidence is not admissible and this is one of them. It normally applies to documents that are at least thirty years old.[7] Professor Simon Greenleaf, our eminent authority in common law evidence, states this rule as follows:

> Every document, apparently ancient, coming from the proper repository or custody, and bearing on its face no evident marks of forgery, the law presumes to be genuine and devolves on the opposing party the burden of proving it to be otherwise.[8]

Simon Greenleaf stipulates that a document comes from the proper custody when it is found in the place where, and under the care of persons whom the writings would naturally be expected to be found. Greenleaf declares one would expect the Gospels to be found in the church in the care of Christians. These sacred writings are so found.

There is the further requirement that the instrument bear on its face no mark of forgery. As mentioned throughout this book, the Gospels present themselves not as forgeries, but as reliable and honest writings from people close to Christ.

For Greenleaf, Montgomery, Chandler and many other legal apologists, there is no doubt that the Gospels — if need be — could be admitted under the 'Ancient Documents Rule'. As is the case with the Gospels, this rule also applies to the copies of lost ancient writings as well as documents that are not signed.[9] The rule is a wise one, because most writers of ancient documents cannot be called to give evidence and their testimony is still needed.

Simon Greenleaf has this to say:

If any ancient document concerning our public rights were lost, copies which had been as universally received and acted upon as the Four Gospels have been, [and] would have been received in evidence in any of our courts of justice, without the slightest hesitation. The entire text of the Corpus Juris Civilis is received as authority in all the courts of continental Europe, upon much weaker evidence of its genuineness.[10]

So the Gospels could be admitted, but does that not simply mean the court is acknowledging their authenticity? Does it also mean the court is taking notice of the (substance) 'story' contained therein? Yes, there are good legal authorities, such as *McCormick on Evidence*, that show that the 'Ancient Documents Rule' applies to the court admitting the contents of the document as well as acknowledging that it exists.[11] The 'Dallas' case and current statute law supports this approach.

In our hypothetical case, the 'story' in the Gospels, not just their authenticity, is important. So, the court could consider the assertions about the historicity of Jesus found in the Gospels, not just find the documents reliable.

Some Christians, even some legal apologists, by their statement that the Gospels are admissible in a court of law, have implied this means all of that which Matthew, Mark, Luke and John record would be received by a modern court.

I believe this is an overstatement. Most courts, especially in the Anglo-American common law tradition, would still evaluate the Gospels carefully following the principle of 'an assertion contained in an ancient document will not be excepted to the hearsay rule if it appears that the declarant would be incompetent to testify if he were present in court.'[12] *In short, only those sections of the Gospels would be admitted where it could be shown that the writer was present at the event he described, reporting on what he knew to be fact from personal observation.*

The rest we call double hearsay and is unlikely to be admitted. In this regard, Luke does not directly indicate he was present at any events he narrates and he writes more as an historian than an eyewitness.[13] Luke's Gospel, written by a paramount historian, would be considered under 'historical knowledge'.

In the chapter on Sir Norman Anderson, we initially focused on the events concerning the death and resurrection of Jesus that Matthew, Peter, John and Paul recorded and were clearly present at. It is those sections of the New Testament that were written by those four and speak of their own observations that would be admissible. And the four personally bear witness to the risen Christ and three to his death. Now, the other Gospel testimony we listed is excellent historically and passes general legal principles. All I am saying is that in a *technical* sense the actual written eyewitness observations of Matthew, Peter, John and Paul is the evidence a modern court would be interested in.

One final observation: the fact that the Creator in his grace has preserved such an abundance of evidence shows he wants no-one to be able to avoid the issue of who Jesus is. The evidence would impress a court of law, but ultimately it amounts to little unless it results in a commitment to Christ and the changed life the risen Lord through the Holy Spirit produces.

Endnotes:

1. Simon Greenleaf, *The Testimony of the Evangelists*, Baker, 1984, pp.7-11 and 53-54; Walter M. Chandler, *The Trial of Jesus from a Lawyer's Standpoint*, I, Federal Book Co., 1925, pp.6-9; John Warwick Montgomery, *Human Rights and Human Dignity*, Zondervan/Probe, 1986, pp.137-139

2. For a more detailed technical discussion on the matters raised in this chapter and this book, see Ross Richard Clifford, *The Case of Eight Legal Apologists for the Defense of Scripture and the Christ Event*, thesis, Simon Greenleaf School of Law, Anaheim, 1987

3. Judicial Notice is to take cognisance of matters which are so clearly established that no formal evidence is necessary. For a discussion on historical knowledge and Judicial Notice, see Sir Rupert Cross, *Evidence*, 5th ed., Butterworths, 1979, pp. 156-159

4. 286 F.2nd 388 (5th Cir. 1961) at 398

5. For similar provisions in other Commonwealth countries, see D. Byrne and J.D. Heydon (eds), *Cross on Evidence*, Butterworths, 1986

6. Adrian Roden QC, a paper entitled 'The Place of Individual Rights in Corruption Investigations', Fourth International Anti-Corruption Conference, Sydney, 16 November 1989, p.19

7. Edward W. Cleary (ed.), *McCormick on Evidence*, 3rd ed., West Publishing, 1984, p.903. And that this rule applies to all documents, therefore including the Gospels, see John Henry Wigmore, *Evidence in Trials at Common Law*, VII, revised by James H. Chadbourn, Little, Brown, 1978, p.743

8. Simon Greenleaf, *op.cit.*, p.7

9. Edward W. Cleary, *op.cit*, p.694 and Francis J. Lamb, *Miracle and Science: Bible Miracles examined by the Methods, Rules and Tests of the Science of Jurisprudence as Administered Today in Courts of Justice*, Bibliotheca Sacra, 1909, pp.26-38

10. Simon Greenleaf, *op.cit*, pp.9-10

11. Edward W. Cleary, *op.cit.*, p.904

12. David F. Binder, *Hearsay Handbook*, 2nd ed., Shepard's/McGraw-Hill, 1983, p.231

13. Luke 1, verses 1 to 4

What the reviewers said:

'This little book will greatly help people understand the strength of the rational case for Christianity. It is written in a clear, interesting style and is eminently suitable for the general reader.'

The Catholic Weekly

'If you have friends who believe that the account of the life of Jesus in the Gospels is a fairy tale, a piece of Jewish mythology, or that Jesus' resurrection was a figment of the disciples' fertile imagination, then this book is a useful broom to be applied to their thinking. It will make them consider again what they have prejudicially dismissed.'

Lawyers Christian Fellowship Newsletter

'The biographical sketches of the lawyers are all interesting, and the evidence and arguments are spelled out clearly with forensic precision.'

Kel Richards, *On Being*

'This is a timely and significant addition to the post-modern debate on the Christ event. In short, in a period of Christian revival, this is a significant book, which every lawyer should read.'

David Kilgour, lawyer, M.P., House of Commons, Canada
Christian Legal Journal

CPSIA information can be obtained
at www.ICGtesting.com
Printed in the USA
FSOW04n1149131117
41120FS